REWARDING PERFORMANCE GLOBALLY

This book provides professionals with an easy reference resource for successfully implementing a performance management system in a multinational company. Providing research-based strategies for reconciling the global-local dilemma is the focus of the book.

The authors explore principles drawn from extensive research in human resources and cross-cultural management. They focus on the critical process of defining, measuring, and rewarding performance in multinational organizations, emphasizing the importance of managing a workforce effectively in today's highly competitive, globalized environment. A real-world case study is woven throughout the book to illustrate further the challenges organizations face when developing strategies, facilitating equivalent and consistent treatment, and contributing to the global mobility of talent.

Rewarding Performance Globally will benefit senior-level HR professionals and will also interest students of international management, human resource management, and cross-cultural management.

Fons Trompenaars is the Founder of the Centre for International Business Studies, a consulting and training organization for international management, which now operates as THT Consulting, the Netherlands.

Robert J. Greene is the CEO of Reward $ystems, Inc. and a Professor in the MBA and MSHR degree programs at DePaul University, USA.

"A timely and comprehensive approach to the challenge of designing effective approaches in a multi-cultural workforce. This book is a must-have for anyone involved in human capital planning and development."

Peter Ronza, *University of Minnesota, USA*

"*Rewarding Performance Globally* provides managers around the world with two dimensions of people management: understanding cultural differences and the difficulties of, and solutions to, rewarding employee performance. While there are many books on cultural differences, none of them take into consideration the difficulties organizations face in designing and implementing rewards and performance systems that can work in diverse cultures. This one solves that problem."

Kathryn McKee, *University of California, Santa Barbara, USA*

"Finally we have thought-provoking treatment of two vital subject areas! The issue of both performance and rewards has been the subjects to many books, but seldom have the two been combined and treated with the global workforce in mind. This book will be of great assistance in coming to appreciate that we need an open mind if we want to succeed, as there is no right or wrong, only what is!"

John S. Maxwell, *Institute for Human Resource Management Education Inc., USA*

REWARDING PERFORMANCE GLOBALLY

Reconciling the Global-Local Dilemma

Fons Trompenaars and Robert J. Greene

Routledge
Taylor & Francis Group
NEW YORK AND LONDON

First published 2017
by Routledge
711 Third Avenue, New York, NY 10017

and by Routledge
2 Park Square, Milton Park, Abingdon, Oxon OX14 4RN

Routledge is an imprint of the Taylor & Francis Group, an informa business

© 2017 Taylor & Francis

The right of Fons Trompenaars & Robert J. Greene to be identified as authors of this work has been asserted by them in accordance with sections 77 and 78 of the Copyright, Designs and Patents Act 1988.

All rights reserved. No part of this book may be reprinted or reproduced or utilised in any form or by any electronic, mechanical, or other means, now known or hereafter invented, including photocopying and recording, or in any information storage or retrieval system, without permission in writing from the publishers.

Trademark notice: Product or corporate names may be trademarks or registered trademarks, and are used only for identification and explanation without intent to infringe.

Library of Congress Cataloging-in-Publication Data
A catalog record for this book has been requested

ISBN: 978-1-138-66902-4 (hbk)
ISBN: 978-1-138-66903-1 (pbk)
ISBN: 978-1-31561-814-2 (ebk)

Typeset in Caslon Pro
by ApexCovantage, LLC

To my grandchildren Joelle, Fons and Johnny since they need
a lot of performance in the global world we created for and
before them
—FT

To recognizing cultural differences, respecting the beliefs of
others and reconciling issues caused by cultural differences
—RG

Contents

LIST OF FIGURES AND TABLES	IX
PREFACE	XIII
ABOUT THE AUTHORS	XV

CHAPTER 1	DETERMINING AN OPTIMAL ORGANIZATIONAL CULTURE	1
CHAPTER 2	CREATING THE DESIRED CULTURE	19
CHAPTER 3	CULTURES THAT FIT A GLOBALIZED CONTEXT	29
CHAPTER 4	RECONCILING UNIVERSALISTIC WITH PARTICULARISTIC PERSPECTIVES	39
CHAPTER 5	RECONCILING INDIVIDUALISTIC WITH COLLECTIVIST PERSPECTIVES	57
CHAPTER 6	RECONCILING NEUTRAL WITH AFFECTIVE PERSPECTIVES	73
CHAPTER 7	RECONCILING SPECIFIC WITH DIFFUSE PERSPECTIVES	81
CHAPTER 8	RECONCILING HIGH-CONTEXT WITH LOW-CONTEXT PERSPECTIVES	91
CHAPTER 9	RECONCILING ACHIEVEMENT WITH ASCRIPTION PERSPECTIVES	99

VIII   CONTENTS

CHAPTER 10 RECONCILING INTERNALLY CONTROLLED
WITH EXTERNALLY CONTROLLED
PERSPECTIVES   105

CHAPTER 11 RECONCILING HIERARCHICAL WITH
EGALITARIAN PERSPECTIVES   117

CHAPTER 12 RECONCILING PAST, PRESENT AND
FUTURE PERSPECTIVES   121

CHAPTER 13 RECONCILING SHORT-TERM WITH
LONG-TERM PERSPECTIVES   125

CHAPTER 14 ACHIEVING CONSENSUS THROUGH
RECONCILIATION   127

CHAPTER 15 SUSTAINING THE EFFECTIVENESS OF
THE CULTURE   137

EPILOGUE   149
INDEX   155

Figures and Tables

Figures

1.1	Four Organizational Cultures	3
1.2	The Eiffel Tower Culture	7
1.3	The Main Characteristics of Organizational Culture Typologies	10
1.4	Contrasts on the Equality–Hierarchical Axis	12
1.5	Six HR Principles	13
1.6	Twenty-four Quadrants for Effective HR Interventions	14
1.7	Quality Circle 1	15
1.8	Quality Circle 2	16
2.1	Performance Management Model	20
2.2	Scale of Thinking vs. Feeling	24
2.3	Thinking/Feeling	25
4.1	The Car and the Pedestrian: Percentage of Respondents Opting for Not Lying in Court and Denying the Friend's Right to Expect to Be Helped	43
4.2	The Global–Local Tension and Its Reconciliation	50
4.3	Learning from Best Practices	51
5.1	Percentage Opting for Individual Freedom—Individual vs. Group Orientation (How to Improve the Quality of Life)	60

FIGURES AND TABLES

5.2 Individual vs. Group Orientation—Percentage of Respondents Who Think Decisions Should Be Made by Compromising   63

6.1 Controlled vs. Expressive—Would You Show Your Emotions Overtly?: Percentage of Respondents Who Would Not Show Their Emotions Overtly at Work   74

7.1 The Danger Zone Between What's Public and What's Private   84

7.2 Percentage Who Would Not Paint the House   89

8.1 Circling Round or Getting Straight to the Point   92

8.2 From the Balanced to the Integrated Scorecard   94

9.1 Doing vs. Being—Quality of Life Is Acting as It Suits You: Percentage of Respondents Who Disagree That One Should Always Act in the Way That Best Suits the Way One Is   101

9.2 Doing vs. Being—Status Comes from Family Background: Percentage of Respondents Who Disagree with the Fact That the Respect a Person Gets Is Highly Dependent on His/Her Family Background   101

10.1 Internal vs. External Control—Making Your Plans Work: Percentage of Respondents Who Think That They Can Make Their Plans Work   107

10.2 Two Examples of the Dangers and Benefits of Balancing the Score Card   115

14.1 Global Organization   128

14.2 Relative Pay Awards Based on Performance   129

14.3 Alternative Distribution Methods from Award Funds   134

E.1 The Yin-Yang of Performance and Rewards Management   153

Tables

2.1	Characteristics of Creative People	23
3.1	Daniels' E-Mail	33
5.1	Implications of Individual vs. Group Orientation for Rewards	61

PREFACE

This book is based on four premises.

The first is that the culture of an organization must be effective and appropriate, given its mission, its environment and its strategy—what works is what fits the context.

The second is that performance and rewards management must facilitate employee alignment with organizational values, be compatible with the context within which the organization functions and facilitate meeting organizational objectives.

The third is that the specific performance and rewards management strategies must fit the various contexts within which work is performed in an organization. A good fit often necessitates customizing strategies to reflect the nature of the work and how that work contributes to organizational success, resulting in different strategies across units and occupations. Readers seeking an in-depth conceptual analysis of the strategy and program alternatives and how they might be applied should consult *Rewarding Performance* by author Greene.

The fourth premise is that strategies must be consistent with the cultural orientation of employees, which is shaped by both societal (national/ethnic) and organizational culture.

Reconciling the so-called global–local dilemma presented by contrasting cultural orientations within the workforce is the challenge that this book addresses. Selecting a global *or* local strategy is not the optimal way to reconcile this dilemma. Rather, a "global through local" strategy must be found in order to truly reconcile the dilemma. This book provides a road map for deciding which principles should be adopted to guide decisions and which strategies should be employed to fit specific contexts. It draws on research and other available and credible evidence to define alternatives for achieving specific objectives and explores contexts in which strategies are likely to be successful. Throughout the book, principles are presented, supplemented by a story line that illustrates how cultural differences can create issues and that provides guidelines for respecting the differences and reconciling the issues.

The book uses examples of potential conflicts when an organization rewards performance for a global workforce. The creation of a culture that enables the organization to set a direction and align its employees' efforts is the first challenge faced. It is then necessary to develop a model that is consistent with the principles of sound performance and rewards management. As organizations go global, they confront the issues raised by cultural differences within the workforce.

About the Authors

Fons Trompenaars earned a PhD from Wharton School, University of Pennsylvania, with a dissertation on differences in conceptions of organizational structure in various cultures. He experienced cultural differences firsthand at home, where he grew up speaking both French and Dutch, and then later at work with Shell  in nine countries. In 1989 he founded the Centre for International Business Studies, a consulting and training organization for international management and now operates as THT Consulting. He has worked as a consultant for Shell, BP, ICI, Philips, Heineken, TRW, Mars, Motorola, General Motors, Nike, Cable and Wireless, CSM and Merrill Lynch. He wrote *Riding the Waves of Culture, Understanding Cultural Diversity in Business*. This book sold over 120,000 copies and was translated into French, German, Dutch, Korean, Danish, Turkish, Chinese, Hungarian and Portuguese. He is also co-author of *Seven Cultures of Capitalism, Building Cross-Cultural Competence* and *21 Leaders for the 21st Century* with Charles Hampden-Turner. Recently he published Riding the Whirlwind, a dynamic new take on creativity and innovation. In 1991 Fons was awarded the International Professional Practice Area Research Award by the American Society for Training and

Development (ASTD). He was mentioned as one of the top 5 management consultants, next to Michael Porter, Tom Peters and Edward de Bono in a leading business magazine in August 1999. In 1994 the translation of his book *Riding the Waves of Culture* was awarded "Book of the Year" by the Order of Experts and Consultants on Organization (OOA), a Dutch management organization.

Robert J. Greene, PhD, SPHR, GPHR, SHRM-SCP, CCP, CBP, GRP is the CEO of Reward $ystems, Inc., a consultancy whose mission is "Helping Organizations Succeed Through People." He is also a faculty member for the MBA and MSHR degree programs for DePaul University. He has over forty years of industry and consulting experience, has authored over 100 articles and the book *Rewarding Performance: Guiding Principles; Custom Strategies*.  He was awarded the first Keystone Award for achieving the highest level of excellence in the field by the American Compensation Association (now World at Work) and has designed professional development programs for numerous associations. He was a principal developer of the PHR and SPHR certifications for the Society for Human Resource Management and the CCP and GRP certifications for World at Work. He holds a PhD from Northwestern U., an MBA from the U. of Chicago and a BA in Economics from U. of Texas–El Paso. Greene has designed and taught certification and professional development programs around the world.

1
DETERMINING AN OPTIMAL ORGANIZATIONAL CULTURE

The most challenging part of workforce management is building and sustaining an effective corporate culture. Culture is often powerful, and it persists when you try to alter it. The key point to remember is that corporate cultures are alive. Like suprahuman organisms, they have their own energy, purpose, direction, values and ways of processing information. Those who believe that cultures can be shaped like clay are in for a surprise. If you attempt to change cultures in a way that violates their sense of order, they will lash back at you. It is a bit like punching a Bobo Doll. It returns to its equilibrium point following any disturbance—and may punch you back! Edgar Schein of MIT has given us what is probably the best definition of corporate culture:

> A pattern of assumptions, invented, discovered or developed by a given group, as it learns to cope with the problem of *external adaptation* and *internal integration*, that has worked well enough to be considered valid, and be taught to new members, as the correct way to perceive, think and feel in relation to these problems.

Schein also recognized a dilemma between "external adaptation" and "internal integration" that must be reconciled.

2 OPTIMAL ORGANIZATIONAL CULTURE

Culture is the pattern by which a group habitually mediates between value differences, such as rules and exceptions, technology and people, conflict and consensus, and so on. Cultures can learn to reconcile such values at ever higher levels of attainment so that better rules are created from the study of numerous exceptions. Successful reconciliations contribute to organizational effectiveness. But in cultures where one value polarity dominates and militates against another, there will be stress, and this will lead to organizational stagnation or disarray.

Given this definition, an example of four types of corporate cultures can be used. They are not only very different, they are polarized. But polarity vs. reconciliation must itself be synergized. Without any initial difference or diversity between people or cultures, there would be nothing to reconcile! Polarities are an essential part of processing information. Distinctions need to be made, and we need to combine them, tolerating these polarities.

Four Corporate Cultures

These cultures vary along two dimensions. Along one dimension, they are more or less egalitarian or hierarchical and more or less oriented to person or to task. But, along the other dimension, this does not mean that cultures with an elite hierarchy set no store by equality. (See Figure 1.1.) Nor are task-oriented cultures completely dismissive of the people who do these tasks. In a very real sense, these four boxes are stereotypes, or archetypes to give them a less opprobrious label. Yet we cannot avoid such labels. They are woven into the mythology and symbolism of all cultures and loom large in the minds of members. Cultures, whether corporate or national, stereotype themselves. For example, the Eiffel Tower, the Sydney Opera House, the Empire State Building are flashed on screens to enable audiences to understand the nature of culture. And films reflect cultural differences, as do other forms of art. When did we ever watch a cowboy hero in an American film whose judgment

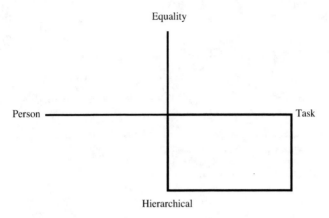

Figure 1.1 Four Organizational Cultures

was overruled by a group? We are still waiting. The individual is always right! There were no awards given for the "Wagon Train of the Year."

The Family Culture

The Family Culture is perhaps the oldest, since a large number of companies originate from family enterprises, even if they eventually go public. On a global scale there are more family owned companies than any other kind. But we are speaking of the Family Culture, not legal ownership. A family may own a company with an Eiffel Tower culture. Or a publicly owned company may have a Family Culture. The Family Culture is hierarchical because the gap between "parents" as owners and "children" as employees is very wide. The "old man" may be revered or feared. He may regard his employees as members of his family, whose burdens he carries. Japanese corporations, even those publicly owned, may pride themselves on "elder brother–younger brother" bonding. Mentoring and coaching are borrowed from the family ideal. MITI, the formidable Japanese government bureaucracy, is nicknamed "Worried Auntie."

The Family Culture is personal rather than task oriented because who you are looms larger than what you do. Family members may not be fully professional. Those most accomplished at tasks may be passed over in favor of the well connected. Insiders have advantages over outsiders. Such cultures are often warm, intimate and friendly, but their internal integration may be achieved at the price of poor external adaptation, and they can "hug and kiss each other into bankruptcy." Creative genius rarely passes down a dynasty, so the vision of the founder may not get renewed in the generations that follow.

The Incubator Culture

Similar to an incubator, this culture is like a leaderless team. This person-oriented culture is characterized by a low degree of both centralization and formalization. In the Incubator Culture, the individualization of all related individuals is one of the most important features. The organization exists only to serve the needs of its members.

The organization has no intrinsic values beyond these goals. The organization is an instrument to serve the specific needs of the individuals in the organization. Responsibilities and tasks within this type of organization are assigned primarily according to the members' own preferences and needs. Structure is loose and flexible, and control takes place through persuasion and mutual concern for the needs and values of other members. Incubator cultures are egalitarian because anyone at any moment, regardless of their status, may come up with a winning idea. They are person-oriented because the tasks necessary to making and distributing these new products are not yet defined. And authority follows expertise rather than title or longevity.

The Guided Missile Culture

The Guided Missile Culture is an egalitarian, task-oriented culture in which project groups steer toward the accomplishment of team

OPTIMAL ORGANIZATIONAL CULTURE

tasks. They are typically multidisciplinary, taking from the various functions of the organization those persons essential for completing their set tasks. They are egalitarian because whose expertise is relevant to their shared problems is an ever open question. NASA was probably the most famous culture of this kind. It took over one hundred disciplines of science and engineering to land people on the moon. The relative contributions of each one had to be negotiated among equals. The only "boss" was the task or mission itself.

This task-oriented culture has a low degree of centralization and a high degree of formalization. This rational culture is in its ideal type both task and project oriented. "Getting the job done" with "the right person in the right place" are favored expressions. Organizational relationships are very results oriented, based on rational/instrumental considerations and limited to specific functional aspects of the persons involved. Achievement and effectiveness are weighted above the demands of authority, procedures or people. Authority and responsibility are placed where the qualifications lie, and they may shift rapidly as the nature of the task changes. Everything in the Guided Missile Culture is subordinated to an all-encompassing goal.

The management of the organization is predominantly seen as a continuous process of solving problems successfully. The manager is a team leader, the commander of a commando unit, in whose hands lies absolute authority. This task-oriented culture, because of its flexibility and dynamism, is highly adaptive but at the same time difficult to manage. Decentralized control and management contribute to the shortness of channels of communication. The task-oriented culture is designed for a rapid reaction to extreme changes. Therefore matrix and project types of organizations are favorite designs.

The Eiffel Tower Culture

This role-orientated culture is characterized by a high degree of formalization, together with a high degree of centralization, and is

OPTIMAL ORGANIZATIONAL CULTURE

symbolically represented by the Eiffel Tower. It is steep, stately and very robust. Control is exercised through a system of rules, legalistic procedures, assigned rights and responsibilities.

Bureaucracy and the high degree of formalization make this organization inflexible. Respect for authority is based on the respect for functional position and status. The bureau or desk has depersonalized authority. Members in an Eiffel Tower culture are continuously subordinated to universally applicable rules and procedures. Employees are very precise and meticulous. Order and predictability are highly valued in the process of managing the organization. Duty is an important concept for an employee in this role-oriented culture. It is the duty one feels within oneself rather than an obligation one feels toward a concrete individual. Procedures for change tend to be cumbersome, and the role-oriented organization is slow to adapt to change.

We all use categorizations like the one just used when defining types of cultures. The point is not to avoid stereotypes—these are everywhere—but to go beyond superficial impressions to see what lies deeper and half submerged. This is what we will be doing with these four quadrants.

The Eiffel Tower culture was described by Max Weber and adopted by Frederick Winslow Taylor and Henry Ford. It is highly structured in the case of a factory processing physical materials, and in the case of a large bureaucracy it does precise, detailed and routine tasks, if possible, without error. Everyone has a precise job description, be it only fixing a wing mirror to a succession of automobiles on an assembly line. These are simple tasks to be done in exactly the way that authorities prescribe. Indeed, the pace of work is dictated by the speed of the moving assembly line. Workers are "machine timed," and every worker must keep up. Such work can be very stressful.

The Hawthorne Experiments were the historic fountainhead of HRM. Do our four quadrants help us make sense of what happened in the case? It should be obvious that scientific management was conceived in the image of the Eiffel Tower. Every worker had his/her task, precisely defined and even calibrated through time-and-motion study. A hierarchy, dominated by a precalculated logic, told the worker what to do, when and at what pace. The worker was considered to be "a pair of hands" (hence a "manual" worker), obeying a strict sequence of orders from superior intelligences, being Taylor and those capable of designing rational and efficient techniques for performing the work. In reality, workers were extensions of big machines, which were far more expensive than they were.

Notice how cultures cooped up in one quadrant of our chart become, over time, half crazed with the potentials of their vision. Taylor himself was neurotic from overcontrol. At night, a machine pressed a cool, wet towel upon his brow. He slept tied by a harness to a tilting bed, lest he roll over and suffer the nightmares that tormented him. Hotels had to be supplied in advance with his paraphernalia for "scientific" sleep. We shall see that to be trapped in any one corner of our chart has potentially catastrophic consequences.

Figure 1.2 depicts the reality of Taylorism and Fordism. It was preponderantly shaped by the culture of the Eiffel Tower, represented

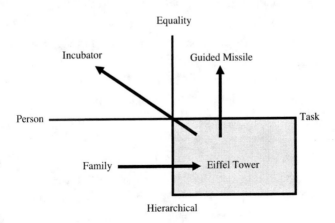

Figure 1.2 The Eiffel Tower Culture

by the shaded square. Note that, even in its extreme form, the Eiffel Tower contains influences from the three other cultures. The designers of this presumably worked as a group in a Guided Missile Culture, perhaps with features of the Family. Almost certainly, they believed they were incubating a "new science." Mass manufacturing, as we know it, is a testament to their efforts, despite its human costs. The constraints were largely imposed on workers rather than on managers.

The arrows pointing to the other quadrants show what the Hawthorne Experiments accomplished, not all of it purposefully! Perhaps the most outstanding changes were triggered accidentally. The Eiffel Tower became a Guided Missile when the women were taken off the factory floor and put in a small group with a shared task, that of becoming more productive. Feedback on their productivity was issued daily, and what today is called a team "scorecard" monitored their progress, allowing them to nudge it steadily upward.

The hypotheses being tested were like the zigzagging of a missile zeroing in on its target. The group developed over time as the women found out more about each other and became friends. This is not individual development so much as an overall rise in the social intelligence of the team, where members felt in control of their destiny. As their productivity climbed and climbed, the number of visitors trying to figure out what was happening increased. The women's combined efforts won them curiosity, respect and approval from authorities. Like modern problem-solving teams, they were bringing enlightenment to those who sponsored them.

The Eiffel Tower was also strongly qualified by a Family Culture. The women became firm friends, baked cakes for one another and became deeply interested in one another's lives. In fact, it became a family atmosphere, which the researchers decided was most responsible for improved performance. The researchers had behaved like permissive parents, not wishing to spoil the experiment by telling the "children" what to do, so the women behaved autonomously before the fond gaze of researchers.

The researchers probably thought they were treating the women "normally." But what is normal among Harvard coresearchers is not normal among foremen and blue-collar workers! After the first two weeks, their regular foreman from the factory floor was forbidden access to them. He was, said the researchers, "upsetting the girls." Hence, their treatment was far more benign than usual. The only permanent institutional change following Hawthorne was a counseling program. Motherly females were hired to provide someone to whom workers could confide if they wished. It was a form of coaching or mentoring but one designed to discharge grievances, not remedy them! It was quietly abandoned in the early sixties.

The final direction in which the Eiffel Tower moved was toward the Incubator Culture at top left of the figure. What was incubated was nothing less than the contemporary values and beliefs of HRM. It is often forgotten that most of what the researchers "discovered" was told to them by the six subjects of the experiment. Credit for this breakthrough belongs as much to the women as to the researchers. They were no longer assembling telephone relays. They were part of an experiment that has opened the eyes of thousands—for experimenting and inquiring is what Incubator Cultures do. They frame hypotheses and look for answers. The fact that the hypotheses in the Hawthorne studies were mostly wrong and were subsequently discarded does not distract from the *inquiring mode*. Indeed, it was because the hypotheses about the effect of environmental conditions (i.e., lighting intensity) were not supported and that productivity continued to rise, that the researchers consulted the six women and gave them veto power over any feature of the experiments they did not like. The researchers became very open to other explanations as their own proved fruitless. The six women were researchers. They were no longer just assembling telephone relays, an activity of mind-numbing boredom. They were *inquiring into how relays might be better assembled.* They were incubating new ways for human beings to work together and learn together.

It is important to grasp that Eiffel Tower Cultures do not just disappear from the landscape. They are no more extinct than volume manufacturing and large bureaucracies. There are still routine, repetitive jobs that need doing, and cost pressures and commoditization mean that it is simply too expensive to run these through groups of experts or spend scarce resources in creating a family atmosphere. All four cultures are necessary to effective organizations. What spells trouble is concentrating exclusively on one quadrant.

We have dealt at some length with the cultural vices of the Eiffel Tower Culture, but all quadrants, if not qualified by other quadrants, will produce ill effects. Consider Figure 1.3.

Few of us like the formality, bureaucracy, mechanization and rigidity of the Eiffel Tower, but are the informality, paternalism,

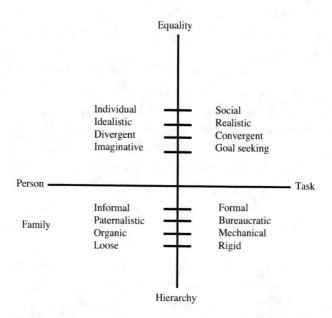

Figure 1.3 The Main Characteristics of Organizational Culture Typologies

organic relations and loose procedures of the Family any better? The seeming warmth and affection of some of these cultures can lure us into complacency, but this does not mean they are soft. They can be fiefdoms of personal power and arbitrary decision. Families have their "feuds and poor relations."

Similarly, many of us feel drawn to the individualism, idealism, imagination and divergent thinking typical of new, incubating companies (top left). Yet their failure rate is extremely high, and their profitability most precarious. Most new start-ups fail. But is the opposite quadrant any better? Are not oversocialization and group think also dangerous? If we converge relentlessly on realistic goals (top right), are we not boxed in, unable to reframe issues or revise tasks?

Cultures Are Patterns of Differences

The eight pairs of values listed in Figure 1.3 show the differences along the two axes of our model. What defines "Individual" is *that to which it has been contrasted*, in this case "Social." The meanings of both values lie not in themselves but in the *differences between them*. They make no sense without this difference. Thus, formality is contrasted with informality, loose with rigid, idealism with realism and so on.

The implication of all this insight is important. *All four quadrants are really differences too.* We will go as mad as Taylor if we try to maximize one end of these continua while avoiding the others. The art of creating a viable corporate culture is to *reconcile* these contrasts or dilemmas, to formalize those informal events that are advantageous, to realize ideals, to diverge in search of new information *and then* converge on a new solution, to be loose and tight by turns.

Because values are really differences, we get a new set of contrasts by reading from top to bottom on the Equality–Hierarchical axis. (See Figure 1.4.)

The four quadrants are recognizable in many ways by anyone familiar with HR. Let us consider (1) Management Style, (2) Power

OPTIMAL ORGANIZATIONAL CULTURE

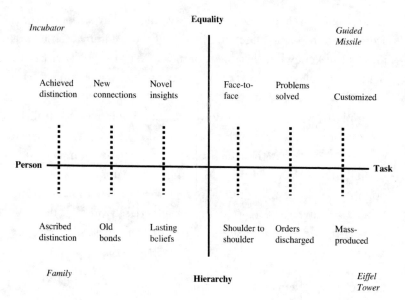

Figure 1.4 Contrasts on the Equality–Hierarchical Axis

Orientation, (3) Source of Cohesion, (4) Principle of Control, (5) Guiding Star and (6) Definition of Excellence. (See Figure 1.5.)

We can also consider what role HR plays in each quadrant so as to:
1. Attract, retain and motivate talent.
2. Reward staff.
3. Set goals and measure performance.
4. Develop staff and leaders.
5. Effect change.
6. Use money to motivate performance.

A glance at these 24 quadrants reveals that an effective HR policy needs to be in *all* of them. If, for example, you wish to retain and motivate talent, then you must hire qualified people, win their trust and loyalty, organize them into teams and get them to fulfill themselves through personal creativity. Depending on the culture, one or

OPTIMAL ORGANIZATIONAL CULTURE

1. Management Style

Management by shared excitement	Management by group goals
Management by mutuality	Management by job description

2. Power Orientation

Power of ideas	Power of knowledge
Power of personality	Power of position

3. Source of Cohesion

Shared breakthrough	Shared mission
Affinity/trust	Common subordination

4. Principle of Control

Authority of science	Authority of solution
Social pressure	Strict rules and procedures

5. Guiding Star

Innovation	Effectiveness
Harmony	Efficiency

6. Definition of Excellence

Creativity/ Genius	Professionalism/ Expertise
Social influence	Level of authority

Figure 1.5 Six HR Principles

more of these quadrants will be more crucial than others, but all are involved in overall HR strategies.

Or consider the most appropriate management style. You start by describing the jobs you wish to fill, but you qualify this with subjective preferences of the jobholders. You then manage by objectives, which are in effect a synthesis of what the organization wants and what employees are professionally committed to achieve. As these achievements become more and more innovative, management by shared excitement becomes possible.

14   OPTIMAL ORGANIZATIONAL CULTURE

Attract, Retain and Motivate Talent

Opportunity for personal creativity/self-actualization	Opportunity to forge team solutions to vital issues
Foster loyalty, sociability, diplomacy, trust	Hire those precisely qualified for job as described

Reward Staff

Learning Creativity Celebration	High esteem among close peers
Personal recognition Special attention	External incentives for exceeding standards

Set Goals and Measure Performance

People render their own jobs more challenging and creative	Teams set more ambitious targets and go on to realize these
The confidence of influential people is won and rapport achieved	Persons come up to standards or fall below these

Develop Staff and Leaders

Ability to turn creative ideas into genuine innovations	Ability to lead, sponsor and/or debrief teams
Read vibes and form fiduciary relationships	Ensure that qualifications match job descriptions

Effect Change

Nurture the creative process Champion innovation	Allow teams to self-organize around company's major issues
Winning the allegiance of key power brokers	Reengineering the workplace to alter its parameters

Use Money to Motivate Performance

A resource to be moved to where the innovation is	A symbol of group and personal achievement Group bonus
A token of mutual respect, a way of caring	Compensation for otherwise exacting work

Figure 1.6 Twenty-four Quadrants for Effective HR Interventions

It is also arguable that many companies pass through phases in which each quadrant becomes the more influential. Suppose you start with a Family Culture at bottom left, as most companies in the world have done, using combined savings as capital. Family members have a brilliantly creative idea that they Incubate (top left). But there is little profit in just generating ideas. These must be turned into products customized to what markets are demanding. This is where the Guided Missile Culture is so appropriate, "guiding" products/services toward customer satisfaction via teams, in a way that makes the customer more effective as a business or a person. It takes a whole team to place products in a rich context of information and service.

Yet markets do inevitably mature. More suppliers are attracted into the industry, margins shrink, profits fall and commoditization sets in. Companies are forced to cut costs and increase volume throughput, which is where the Eiffel Tower comes back to haunt us! Guided Missile cultures are too expensive for commodity-type output. Track this course in Figure 1.7.

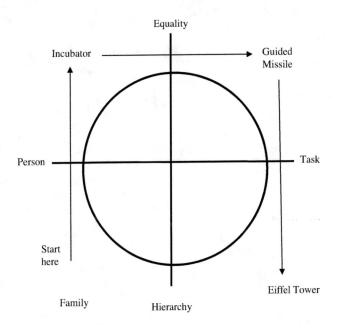

Figure 1.7 Quality Circle 1

But even if a company comes full circle, the Eiffel Tower should be supported by the other quadrants. Quality Circles are ways of punctuating routine production work with Guided Missile deliberations. Routine work can take on an important new meaning, provided employees are testing new ideas and reorganizations of their own workplaces. It is even possible to incubate new ideas in Quality Circles and discover their validity by trying these out in the factory or the office in the days following. Having an Eiffel Tower organization does *not* stop employees thinking, discovering and learning, as W. Edwards Deming and his cycles of Continuous Improvement demonstrate. He prescribed the sequence of act-plan-implement-check, which fits fairly well into our four quadrants. (See Figure 1.8.)

An organization learns by using all four quadrants, even when one culture looms larger than the others. If incubation is not

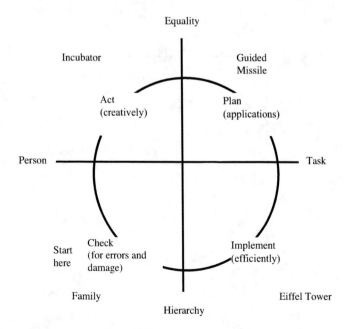

Figure 1.8 Quality Circle 2

connected to the efficient manufacture and marketing of finished products and services, *where are the profits to sustain its creativity going to come from?* Every quadrant needs the others to sustain it. Do not trap yourself in the alchemist's dream of creating gold from base metals—or in Taylor's tilting bed.

International Variation in Preferred Corporate Cultures

One serious mistake is to assume that the culture preferred in the domestic HQ of an international company will work throughout the world and that HR can globalize its various tools without serious problems.

One reason why the Incubator Culture is so rarely the preferred one is that creative persons are a small minority in all cultures, so that using national aggregates tends to hide this preference. Richard Florida, in *The Rise of the Creative Class*, reveals that America's astonishing burst of creativity in the last decade of the twentieth century derives from less than 15% of its working population and is confined to a dozen or so urban centers across the U.S. This 15% produces 85% of successful innovations and has transformed America's fortunes and restored the nation to industrial leadership.

But the methods used to reward employees in task-oriented cultures like those in the U.S. may fail dismally in person-oriented cultures. Why should I be paid for my performance when I owe all success to the support of my Family, especially my warm, inspiring teacher and boss? Is it not insulting to him and my wonderful colleagues to pretend I did it all myself? How embarrassing to be elected Employee of the Month when my team has done so much to help and sustain me? "I think I'll call in sick!" "How do you want me to fill in this time sheet?" "Describe the activity I spent the time on as, 'Tried out several ideas and abandoned them all.'"

The effectiveness or not of HR tools depends very much on the corporate culture of that nation and locality. No "universal" measures can retain exactly the same meanings across cultures.

There is no mistaking what most of the employees we talk to prefer as a culture. Across the globe, they have their eyes on that almost empty top-left quadrant, the Incubator. They vary considerably on what is real for them and the corporate culture they now inhabit, but they vary less in what is ideal. Nearly every senior manager we talk to and test seeks to be more creative and innovative—wants the corporation to renew itself.

An HR department that can create the opportunities to reach this idealized goal, especially among the restless migrants of Generation X, is going to win the war for talent, recruiting, assessing, retaining and fulfilling the best employees.

2
CREATING THE DESIRED CULTURE

Organizations will generally need to find a blend of the strengths of all of these culture types. For example, one could create an Incubator Culture that has a Family management style and yet still gain some of the benefits of becoming more Guided Missile–like and adopting some of the positive aspects of an Eiffel Tower Culture. This approach can prevent suffering from some of the shortcomings of a Family Culture, which could happen if management behaves like benevolent parents. There is a need to make employees believe the executives feel an obligation to provide all the benefits of employment they could while remaining fiscally responsible.

And there is a need to define, measure and reward performance in a dynamic manner, changing as the culture of the organization changes and as the business goes through its evolution. Initially, it is necessary to develop a performance model for the organization that fits the current culture and context. A conceptual framework for aligning the performance model with the culture and the context is shown in Figure 2.1.

It may be appropriate for the present culture to have characteristics of the Family Culture but also be complemented by a dose of Guided Missile to align efforts and a touch of Eiffel Tower to maintain the course heading. But it may also need to be very Incubator-like, so that the needed products can be invented and the

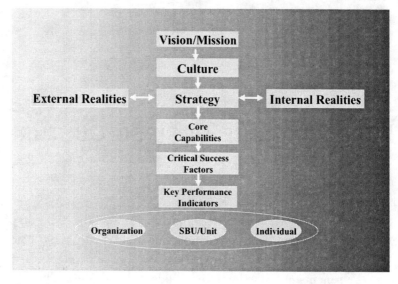

Figure 2.1 Performance Management Model

ways to penetrate the target markets created. How the organization defines, measures and rewards performance will have a major impact on success. If the proper objectives are identified and incentives put in place to motivate employees, it is likely that they will focus on the key performance indicators and critical success factors, increasing the chances that employees will be engaged in the business and will experience a sense of meaningfulness in their work.

And it may be necessary to create subcultures within the organization, enabling the local culture to fit the objectives, the type of work and the type of people who do it. Measuring and rewarding performance quantitatively in sales and production may be the best fit, while in staff functions, it might be done very differently. Having a more Guided Missile Culture in sales, while other parts of the organization are in Incubator or Eiffel Tower Cultures, is appropriate, as long as the organization can manage this so that synergistic benefits accrue to the organization.

CREATING THE DESIRED CULTURE 21

Once the appropriate cultures are defined and put into place, the next step is to develop definitions of performance and to implement incentive plans that ask for and reward the right results, while exhibiting the right behaviors. And the incentives may differ across functions, with sales incentives targeted at generating revenue, while incentives for operating units may be focused on quality and cost. But consideration must be given also to create incentives that encourage a "shared destiny" mind-set among all employees. One approach is to use equity to reward overall results, since the share price or valuation will be impacted by the performance of all functions. "People don't wash rental cars" is a concept worthy of consideration.

So employees can receive their current cash compensation based on different criteria and delivered differently while all share in the same overarching plan tied to organizational results. This has a Family Culture dimension but can also promote a Guided Missile type of culture as well.

As start-up/emerging organizations grow, the culture will often need to be reshaped to be more of a Guided Missile type and to consider adopting some of the structure that fits an Eiffel Tower Culture. The trick is to move from one to the other at the right time and not to throw out the good during transitions. Many start-ups were launched like rockets but failed in their missions because the fuel supply was inadequate or the navigation was inappropriate. Families became incestuous . . . Incubators turned into unruly mobs . . . Guided Missiles were so focused on tasks and goals they forgot they were dealing with people . . . and Eiffel Towers with brilliant structures were immovable when the game changed. One of the biggest challenges is to define, measure and reward performance in a manner that is consistent with the current culture but that also acts as a vehicle to propel the organization to a culture that is appropriate for its mission, objectives and the environment going forward into the future.

22   CREATING THE DESIRED CULTURE

In order to move forward, an organization needs to be sure it has the right people in place. Defining, measuring and rewarding performance in a manner that fits the desired culture can be effective but only if the workforce is qualified to do what is needed and is committed to our mission and objectives. This requires that the organization attract and retain a pool of human capital that fits what is required. One way to do this is to develop a brand as an employer and then to formulate a staffing and development strategy that will get and keep the workforce it needs.

An organization's culture is extremely important in defining who and what it is, so potential employees can decide whether it is a good fit for them. There is compelling research that supports the use of *realistic job previews* (RJPs) when recruiting and selecting new employees. The research shows that the RJPs are the most effective way to avoid unwanted turnover during the first one to two years, since they begin the relationship on an honest basis and also inoculated recruits against the not so great things they are bound to face in a new organization. So when an organization develops a clear brand, it can use that to make decisions about how well candidates fit the culture and enable candidates for employment to make similar assessments.

Tools for assessing candidate personalities can be useful in making "good fit" determinations. THT Consulting has created a tool that is available on their website. If an organization is at a stage of development where the critical knowledge/skills that are most needed are in the product development area, its challenge is to find people who are able to be creative in the innovation of new products. Competitors are attempting to mimic the existing products, and since there is no practical way to stop them, the best approach is to stay a step ahead. THT has defined characteristics that creative people tend to have and not to have. (See Table 2.1.)

THT has done research indicating that creative people move more effectively *between* intuition and thinking, that innovators

CREATING THE DESIRED CULTURE 23

Table 2.1 Characteristics of Creative People

Creative people are more . . .	Creative people are less . . .
Intuitive	Sensing
Perceiving	Judging
Thinking	Feeling
Extroverted	Introverted
Tortoise brained	Hare brained
Lateral	Focused
Risk taking	Securing
Hunting	Gathering
Individualistic	Consensus seeking
Right brained	Left brained
Etc.	Etc.

extrovertly publish their introverted calculation and constantly learn by oscillating *between* judging and perceiving, and that they finally check their feelings *through* thinking. An additional finding is that culture often determines the side that respondents start from. This does not mean that one culture is more creative than another but that their starting point for looking at a problem is different. Not combining opposite logics shows an absence of creativity. Clapping with one hand makes little noise.

One of the fundamental concerns THT has with the classic profiling tools is that each dimension is based on the single-axis continuum. The logic behind this tools asks whether you are sensing *or* intuiting? The *more* you identify yourself as Sensing, the *less* you must be of the Intuiting type. When seeking to apply this typology or, indeed, any other associative model in an international context, accretion to the extremities of each scale is constraining. Despite professional psychologists' discussion of preference with reference to the dominance of the right or left hand when writing, it remains a poor solution. Both could be used, but one is usually dominant. Whereas this model is applicable in explaining hand preferences when writing, it hardly helps one when clapping. During applause, it doesn't really matter which hand is dominant, but success will depend on the coordination between both the hands.

Although users of single-axis tools do talk about combining the variety of preferences in teams and organizations, one cannot derive this approach from the basic instrument as it is based on forced choice bimodal questions. Much of the of research on creativity owes its origin to Anglo-Saxon or North American thinking, even though it has been "exported" across the world. If people utilize other types of logic, such as Ying-yang or Taoism, the realization that profiling on bimodal dimensions is questionable. THT has applied a new logic.

To test the preference for thinking or feeling, a forced choice question, such as the following, is usually asked:

1. "I like to subject a problem to rational thought and logical analysis. Wishing something were true does not make it so. Feelings are not 'wrong.' They're irrelevant."
2. "I always ask myself what I feel about a problem because 'the heart has its own reasons which Reason knows not of.' I seek to develop emotional muscles."

Thus with a series of such questions, the investigator is trying to place the individual on the scale of thinking vs. feeling. (See Figure 2.2.)

How the respondent answers these questions gives insight into when the dominant culture in which it is applied prefers decisiveness or being consulted. But what if, in a multicultural environment, one finds people with different opinions? The decisive leader will agonize over the fact that many want to go for consensus. Conversely, the sensitive leader will not succeed because of an apparent

Figure 2.2 Scale of Thinking vs. Feeling

CREATING THE DESIRED CULTURE

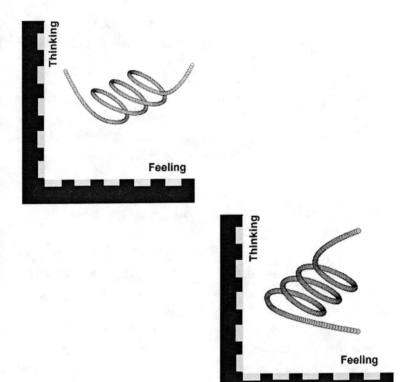

Figure 2.3 Thinking/Feeling

lack of decisiveness. Thus there is a dilemma between the seemingly opposing orientations of Thinking *or* Feeling.

Charles Hampden-Turner shows how seemingly opposing things can be reconciled with his meta-level Dilemma Theory. Thus the addition of two alternative options provides a means of evaluating the individual's propensity to reconcile this dilemma (see Figure 2.3.):

3. "I like to subject a problem to rational thought and logical analysis. Yet feats of intelligence or folly arouse feelings within me, so these too guide my intelligence."

4. "I always ask myself what I feel about a problem because my boredom, irritation or excitement is an early clue as to whether I can engage intelligently and find a solution."

Those who answer "3"are starting from a Thinking orientation but accounting for the Feeling of others. They have successfully reconciled the opposites. This process involves starting from one axis and spiraling to the top right, and thus the individual has integrated both components.

Similarly, those who answer "4" are starting from Feeling but spiraling toward Thinking, again integrating the two seemingly opposite orientations.

In THT's model, called the ITI (Integrated Type Indicator), the questions represent the two extreme opposing values for each conjugate pair. However, they also add two additional choices that represent the clockwise and anticlockwise reconciliation between these extremes. By combining the answers from a series of questions in this extended format, a profile can be computed that reveals the degree to which an individual seeks to integrate the extreme dimensions.

Each variable is scaled from 0 to 10 by combining responses to these extended questions. A typical ITI profile could then be $I^9e^3N^6s^2T^9f^1P^8j^7$ compared to the standard **INTP** description.

Then the overall propensity to reconcile (= an index between 0 and 100) is:

(Introvert + Extrovert) + (Sensing + Intuiting) + (Thinking + Feeling) + (Judging + Perceiving) ÷ 4 = Developing Creativity Potential

THT has found that this model has already generated insights over and above profiles based on the traditional four linear scales. The key finding was that simply rejecting opposite orientations will

CREATING THE DESIRED CULTURE   27

get you nowhere. Abandoning your own extreme and adopting the other extreme is like trying to impress your first date by acting out an unfamiliar role—you'll soon be found out.

The integrated approach enables an organization to determine an individual's propensity for reconciling dilemmas, as a direct measure of creativity, an ability that could be termed *innovative competence.* It transcends the single culture in which it may be measured and so provides a robust, generalizable model for all environments. Reconciliation is the real essence of the creative individual. The THT approach is different from the classic M-B because it is underpinned by the recognition that, while managers work to accomplish this or that separate objective, creative leaders deal with *the dilemmas of seemingly "opposed" objectives, which they continually seek to reconcile.*

So, instead of questions that are based on linear (Likert) scales, the THT *integrated innovation indicator* asks questions in the following format:

Q1 Which of the following four options best describes how you most frequently behave?

   a) I am efficient, thorough, adaptable, methodical, organized, precise, reliable and dependable. (5 score in invention, 0 score in adaptation, 0 score in innovation)

   b) I am ingenious, original, independent, unconventional and unpredictable. (0 score in invention, 5 score in adaptation, 0 score in innovation)

   c) I am continuously checking in an organized and methodical manner whether my original ideas do work in practice. (5 score in invention, 0 score in adaptation, 8 score in innovation)

   d) I am methodical and organized first, to set the basis to launch my unconventional ideas. (0 score in invention, 5 score in adaptation, 8 score in innovation)

3
CULTURES THAT FIT A GLOBALIZED CONTEXT

When organizations begin to globalize, issues associated with a culturally diverse workforce arise. Even though an organization might have created a culture that fits its context and contributes to its performance, a culturally diverse workforce presents additional challenges. In order for employees to be motivated to contribute to organizational success, they must feel how business is conducted and how they are treated fit their beliefs, values and priorities. Doing business across borders of course creates legal, logistical and economic issues. Those issues are dealt with in other works. The focus of this book is to recognize the issues created by a culturally diverse workforce.

Even if an organization has all of its employees in one country, the increasingly mobile workers have contributed to culturally diverse workforces. If you don't go there, they will come here. Coauthor Greene was working at a NASA site, advising the organization on employee compensation strategy. He asked lab management whether they wished to consider how cultural diversity would impact the acceptance of programs by employees; the response was that all employees were in one location in California. Yet when one walked through the campus, it looked very much like a UN meeting. And discussions with scientists and engineers confirmed

29

that they brought their cultural heritages with them, creating challenges for the organization to satisfy everyone that they were being rewarded appropriately.

"Going there" with operations certainly creates enormous challenges for an organization. The question is whether management feels they can manage a part of their organization that is thousands of miles away, operating in a time zone that is 12 hours off theirs. The early afternoon conference calls from headquarters will mean others will be trying to form sentences in the wee hours of the morning—and do so with language and cultural differences impeding phone or teleconference communication. This can stretch the management capabilities of any organization. And selling the organization's preferred culture to people with widely different views about how they should be managed can be enormously difficult. This is particularly true if the organization has an ethnocentric bias. In the U.S., children are told to treat others as *you* would like to be treated. But in today's globalized world, that principle should be to treat others as *they* would like to be treated.

Most multinationals use expatriates heavily to staff key positions in the early stages of operations outside the headquarters country. Expatriates who have been socialized to the headquarters culture can be expected to behave predictably in foreign operations. But the cost of having a large number of people in international postings can become burdensome. And increasingly countries are imposing limits on granting work visas to employees who are not host country citizens. So the challenges associated with finding workforce management strategies that will work everywhere appear early and often have a major impact on the success of foreign operations.

As mentioned earlier, how an organization defines, measures and rewards performance will have a major impact on workforce effectiveness. This key business process needs to fit the organization's culture. But it also needs to be viewed by employees as appropriate.

CULTURES THAT FIT A GLOBALIZED CONTEXT   31

The decision as to whether it is done consistently globally or customized locally is a critical one.

In order to explore how an organization-wide system for defining, measuring and rewarding performance might be received across countries, a case study will be used. Although the case is fictional, it incorporates issues that have been encountered by many organizations and illustrates the potential impact of national/ethnic cultural diversity. It is important to note that, although the characters may seem to be stereotypes that are commonly assumed for people from different countries, the purpose is not to imply that Frenchmen, for example, have one homogeneous culture, while Italians have another very different homogeneous culture. Trompenaars and others have found that some Frenchmen will behave more like Italians than some Italians. This implies a considerable intraculture diversity and interculture overlap. However, considerable cross-cultural research by Trompenaars, Hofstede, Triandis and others has shown tendencies for national/ethnic cultures to possess characteristics at an aggregate level. So it is legitimate to expect people from China to be likely to have different cultural profiles than those from the U.S. It is, however, incumbent on those acting on these assumptions to attempt to determine the cultural orientation of individuals, lest they be lumped into a broad category that does not fit them.

Case Study: Qwenchy International

The Global Director of Human Resources has called a meeting of the country HR managers. The meeting is intended to reach agreement on the introduction of a new performance and reward management system. The system would be one that is mutually acceptable to different countries in which Qwenchy operates. The organization wishes to build a case that demonstrates how one can benefit from cultural variety yet utilize management systems that are consistent across Qwenchy.

"Cultural diversity does not always lead to misunderstandings and problems: It also forms a huge opportunity for gaining competitive advantage," argues the Global HR Director in an e-mail to the group of people who will serve as a task force evaluating the new approach. He continues:

> You are to attend an important meeting called to discuss and decide upon the introduction of a new Performance and Rewards Management system. The participants will be the Country Human Resource Managers. At the end of the meeting, you have to present an outline of a mutually acceptable system that can be deployed globally. You are expected to make a useful contribution and help the group reach its decisions by contributing your ideas on all topics.
>
> Today Qwenchy is a global organization. The manufacturing, R&D, HR and Finance activities are coordinated by Headquarters in the U.S. The regional marketing responsibilities are decentralized to your regions, although individual countries operate within centralized constraints concerning logos, letterhead, type of products and financial criteria. Our corporate HR function is centralized in the U.S. office and looks after consistency in labor conditions, job classification and personnel planning throughout the regional subsidiaries. Recruitment of personnel is done by you in the regional offices.
>
> Confronted with fierce competition, top management has done much to revitalize its whole business

CULTURES THAT FIT A GLOBALIZED CONTEXT 33

Table 3.1 Daniels' E-Mail

Qwenchy International		
Date	:	29 October 2014
Subject	:	Meeting to introduce a new Performance and Rewards Management System
From	:	J. A. Daniels
To	:	National Human Resource Directors
		Mr. Yakomoto Qwenchy International Japan
		Mr. Mantovani Qwenchy International Italy
		Mr. Klaus Qwenchy International Germany
		Mr. Khasmi Qwenchy International UAE-Dubai
		Ms. Jones Qwenchy International USA

approach. Part of this new approach is the discussion about the implementation of a new Performance and Rewards Management System for the entire company. I am e-mailing you a memo that explains the thinking of senior management about how we manage our workforce (Table 3.1). Please familiarize yourselves with its content and be prepared to discuss it when you meet here at headquarters.

Dear Country HR Directors:

I am happy to invite you to a "brainstorming-meeting" on the introduction of our new Performance and Rewards Management System. Until recently, performance and rewards management has been done on a relatively ad hoc basis, with local customs impacting actual processes. But times have changed. Motivated employees are in danger of being lost due to growing competition for top talent. Increasingly, we realize that staff appraisal and competitive rewards should be the cornerstone of our company's Human Resources policy. Indeed, employee engagement can best be attained by increasing employee motivation and by rewarding results and contributions appropriately. One of the strongest motivational forces is the linkage between individual performance and rewards. Therefore, one of the main principles built into our new system should be pay for performance. It is my belief that this is vital to guarantee the continuity of our company. We must recognize that how effectively, competitively and appropriately we define, measure and reward performance will impact the quality of our workforce and out success. What I consider to be an ideal system for Qwenchy International comprises the following elements:

I Values

Entrepreneurship within Qwenchy International means recognizing that our performance relies on the motivation, commitment and expertise of our employees. People are a vital factor in Qwenchy's business, and people management is crucial to our success. Therefore, this new system is to become management's primary instrument for guiding and steering our employees.

II Clear Goals

The main purpose of the appraisal process is to improve performance. The main purpose of introducing pay for performance is to motivate staff.

III Clear Criteria for What Is Being Appraised

- Individual targets should be set at the start of the appraisal period, and performance should be reviewed regularly against fixed criteria, such as key results achieved, effectiveness in reaching targets and contribution to business plans.

CULTURES THAT FIT A GLOBALIZED CONTEXT   35

- Criteria should be established that will be used to measure competencies, such as performance under pressure, influencing others, safety awareness, effective planning, ability to defend opinions firmly and sense of reality.

IV   Clear and Consistent Guidelines for the Appraisal Process

- Scheduling of appraisal meetings.
- Preparation and procedures for appraisal meetings.
- Documenting the outcome of the appraisal meeting using the Staff Appraisal Form.

V   Strong Links to Procedures for Promotion and Rewards

I feel strongly about introducing an individualized system of pay for performance; that is, I want financial rewards to be dependent on individual contribution to business results. I believe this type of reward system is one of the strongest motivating forces imaginable. Obviously, the recent financial crisis has shown we should not base rewards solely on short-term financial results that employees cannot influence, but this does not mean we should not sharply differentiate between high and low performers.

It is my intention to introduce the new system in exactly the same way in all countries in which Qwenchy operates. I believe that we need a centralized and standardized approach to staff appraisal. If we use any other approach, we risk losing consistency. We will also lose the opportunity to move people around. Hence we will use only one standard Staff Appraisal Form worldwide. The objective of having your group discuss the process is that it is important that the process is the same in all the countries we operate in and that the process will work well in all countries.

At the end of the meeting, I expect to have an outline of a system that is feasible and that is acceptable to all of us. I welcome as many recommendations and suggestions as possible.

I enclose a list of Ten Principles Leading to Effective Staff Appraisal that I have always found personally useful.

I look forward to your input.

J. A. Daniels

Ten Principles Leading to Effective Staff Appraisal

We incorporate a number of principles into the instructions that will be sent to all appraisers globally for the next staff appraisal round.

Please read them carefully, I have always felt them to be most useful. I would be very happy to hear your comments.

1. The appraisal should focus on appraising *specific results* of the individual as output and individual *function-specific behavior* as input.
2. Judgments should be based on *performance and business results* and not be misled by any kind of personal preference. The appraisal should not be biased by prejudices or personal characteristics.
3. Each appraisal criterion should be evaluated in *isolation*, without letting strong or weak points of the appraisee influence the evaluation of other criteria.
4. Ratings should not be influenced by previous experiences with the appraisee (a recent success or blunder should not bias the actual appraisal).
5. Evaluation should be on the basis of *this year only*. Past performances should not be taken into account.
6. Judgments should be based on *concrete facts*, not on notions or assumptions. The appraisal must be as *objective* as possible.

CULTURES THAT FIT A GLOBALIZED CONTEXT   37

7. Low ratings must be given when appropriate. A boss who always tries to stay in the safe middle is doing injustice to other well performing employees and/or tolerating poor performance.
8. Evaluations should be on the basis of *fair company norms*, even if the requirements of the job are not well-defined and performance is difficult to measure.
9. Evaluators should be *honest, open, frank and direct*, and not afraid of confrontations.
10. Ranking procedures for determining rewards are *consistent* with the actual appraisal. The Staff Appraisal Form should justify the salary increases.

4
RECONCILING UNIVERSALISTIC WITH PARTICULARISTIC PERSPECTIVES

The Qwenchy dialogue began. Daniels opened the meeting and welcomed all country HR representatives. He then turned the meeting direction over to Ms. Jones, the Director of HR Operations and left to attend another meeting. She started by suggesting:

> Obviously, I am very satisfied with Mr. Daniels' proposal. I want the group to reach agreement, but I am quite sure that Mr. Daniels has outlined an ideal system. In other words, I would be quite disappointed if you, my dear colleagues rejected the idea of a universal and standardized system. I believe you would be well advised to stick to the proposal. In the U.S. it works so well; why shouldn't it work in other countries? Only if you come up with reasonable arguments will I be open to compromise. I hereby open the meeting and hope we have fruitful discussions. Do you have any questions?

The Italian representative, Mr. Mantovani, was flabbergasted. He is against the idea of introducing any system worldwide in a

40 UNIVERSALISTIC/PARTICULARISTIC PERSPECTIVES

standardized form. He reacted: "Ms. Jones, with all due respect for the professionalism of you and Mr. Daniels, I think that the cookie cutter approach might work well on our pizzas but not on humans. In Italy we are concerned about a humane approach that respects each employee, not treating them as robots." "Yes," Mr. Khasmi added, "although we are not against having standardized, worldwide system, I think it is wise to attune some aspects to the traditions and values of local operating companies, We need to respect our religious environment, as well as our local cultures. Can we create some room for local adaptation"?

Ms. Jones responded by saying that some adaptations were likely around the conceptual framework offered by Mr. Daniels. As long as the main philosophy was untouched, some local adaptations were permitted.

Mr. Klaus from Germany made it clear that he is particularly serious about one issue: The appraisee should also be evaluated on his/her compliance with the rules, procedures and regulations stipulated by the organization. "As long as we see clarity in the procedures and the way we need to apply them at home, I don't see any problems."

The Japanese representative Yakomoto-san didn't think it was feasible to standardize the system worldwide. He expressed himself clearly and with diplomacy: "Each culture is different and has different ways of solving problems. For example, the so-called Ten Principles would be totally counterproductive when applied to our country. How can you isolate a person from his or her job? How can you evaluate on the basis of this year only? Should you not take efforts and progress into account? What are concrete facts? Do they exist? How can they expect us to be direct and confrontational? Let's take these aspects into consideration as well."

Ms. Jones was shaking her head after this first encounter with her colleagues. But nothing was lost. There was at least an open spirit and a subscription to the values that Daniels had communicated.

Universalistic vs. Particularistic Perspectives

What happened during the initial meeting was what one would expect when people from diverse cultures meet. But differences in perspective can lead to a better and more practical result, assuming participants are willing to protest HQ's proposals that they know don't work in their local environments. One of the most fundamental dimensions of culture is universalism vs. particularism, which is very much in evidence in the Qwenchy kickoff meeting.

The universalistic vs. particularistic dimension of culture deals with an orientation to having one set of rules for everyone (universalistic) or varying the application of rules based on who the parties are or the circumstances (particularistic). People with a universalistic orientation believe that who the person is should not influence how rules are interpreted, and they resist practices such as preferential hiring of friends or relatives (which they often call "nepotism" and often have policies forbidding it). These consistency-oriented cultures assume that what is good and right can be defined and always applies, regardless of the person in question. Much attention is given to abstract societal or organizational codes that every individual should stick to.

Universalistic perspectives are most common in Western countries, such as the U.S. But those with a particularistic orientation believe that circumstances or who the individual is should result in a flexible application of rules and policies, and they resist bureaucratic processes. These flexible cultures focus on the obligations of relationships and requirements posed by unique circumstances. Friendship implies special obligations, which take priority over abstract codes. There is no one good way that must always be followed—it depends. Particularistic cultures are more common in countries of South America, Latin Europe, Asia and the Middle East.

The following is a series of considerations that one could take into account to distinguish between more rule- and exception-oriented people.

42 UNIVERSALISTIC/PARTICULARISTIC PERSPECTIVES

Do we focus on abstract ideas about what is right? On standards and rules that:

- Apply to everybody.
- Oblige people to behave in certain ways.
- Successfully regulate behavior.
- Ensure equality so that we treat all people in the same way.

Or do we focus on particular obligations to the people he or she knows? For example:

- Differences in how we are obligated to people.
- The exceptional nature of the present circumstances.
- On our specific relationship to people—as friends, brothers, colleagues or parents—rather than as fellow citizens?
- On their unique importance to us, with their special claims on our love or attention.
- My obligation to sustain, protect and support them, no matter what the rules say.

How Do We Test This Difference in Perspective?

The following situation, developed by Stouffer and Toby, takes the form of a dilemma that exists between the two orientations (Question 1 of the cross-cultural questionnaire IAP).[1]

You are riding in a car driven by a close friend. He hits a pedestrian.

You know he was going at least 45 miles per hour in an area of the city where the maximum allowed speed is 30 miles per hour. There are no witnesses. His lawyer says that if you testify under oath that he was only driving 30 miles per hour it may save him from serious consequences.

What right has your friend to expect you to protect him?

> *1a) My friend has a definite right as a friend to expect me to testify to the lower figure.*

UNIVERSALISTIC/PARTICULARISTIC PERSPECTIVES   43

1b) He has some right as a friend to expect me to testify to the lower figure.
1c) He has no right as a friend to expect me to testify to the lower figure.

What do you think you would do in view of the obligations of a sworn witness and the obligation to your friend?

1d) Testify that he was going 30 miles an hour.
1e) Not testify that he was going 30 miles an hour.

Figure 4.1 shows how many people from a variety of nationalities answered that the friend had some right or no right and that they would not testify in court in the friend's favor (i.e., Answers 1b–c and 1e).

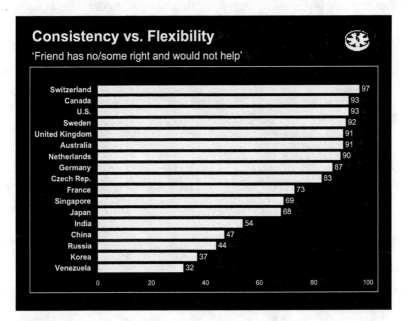

Figure 4.1 The Car and the Pedestrian: Percentage of Respondents Opting for Not Lying In Court and Denying the Friend's Right to Expect to Be Helped (Answers 1b-c and 1e)

44 UNIVERSALISTIC/PARTICULARISTIC PERSPECTIVES

Key Findings

- North Americans and most North Europeans emerge as almost totally consistent in their approach to the problem.
- The proportion falls to under 72% for French and Japanese respondents and to under 33% in Venezuela—the majority would lie to the police to protect their friend.
- Through informal discussions in our workshops, THT Consulting found that responses diverge even further when we ask participants to imagine the pedestrian had died. Consistency-oriented people become even more hesitant to help their friend, while flexibility-oriented cultures say they would then definitely testify in the friend's favor.

In practice, we use both kinds of judgment, one to reinforce the other. Imagine, for example, that a female employee is being harassed in the workplace. The difference in disapproval is one in terms of weight and ordering, not one in terms of mutual exclusion:

Consistency-Focused Disapproval

- Harassment is immoral and against company rules. It must have been a terrible experience for Jennifer and really upset her.

Flexibility-Focused Disapproval

- Jennifer must have experienced a great deal of distress. No women in our company should have to deal with harassment in the workplace.

There are limitations in the earlier car accident question. Although the question has the advantage of forced choice, it causes respondents to reflect on the dilemma—and how they would approach it. It enables us to place individuals along the bipolar scale; however, it does not tell us anything about how individuals respond to the dilemma with regard to how they might reconcile the opposing

UNIVERSALISTIC/PARTICULARISTIC PERSPECTIVES 45

choices. In order to assess their personal responses, we have therefore extended the original forced-choice questions to include options to reject reconciliation, to compromise, and to reconcile from the universal to the particular or from the particular to the universal.

THT's research done over the last 25 years was very much based on finding preferences of groups but didn't look into the so-what? question. And it also didn't look at possible combinations of helping friends and telling the truth. We developed an alternative set of options.

The Car and the Pedestrian

You are a passenger in a car driven by a close friend. He hits a pedestrian.

You know he was going at least 35 miles per hour in an area of the city where the maximum speed allowed is 20 miles per hour. There are no witnesses. His lawyer says that if you are prepared to testify under oath that he was only driving at 20 miles per hour, it may save him from serious consequences.

How would you act in this case?

1. *There is a general obligation to tell the truth as a witness. I will not perjure myself before the court. Nor should any real friend expect this from me.*
2. *There is a general obligation to tell the truth in court, and I will do so, but I owe my friend an explanation and all the social and financial support I can organize.*
3. *My friend in trouble always comes first. I am not going to desert him before a court of strangers based on some abstract principle.*
4. *My friend in trouble gets my support, whatever his testimony, yet I would urge him to find in our friendship the strength that allows us both to tell the truth.*
5. *I will testify that my friend was going a little faster than the allowed speed and say that it was difficult to read the speedometer.*

46 UNIVERSALISTIC/PARTICULARISTIC PERSPECTIVES

With these selections, we can assess both the cultural orientation of the individual in the way they approach dilemmas (more universalistic or more particularistic) and their propensity to reconcile them.

The central aim of this book is to help readers to improve and develop their ability to deal with dilemmas at both the personal level (dilemmas faced when working with other people) and at the organizational level. As we've said, the capacity to reconcile dilemmas is how we define intercultural leadership competence and is a direct measure of leadership potential relevant to the twenty-first century.

By combining questions that follow the logic of the preceding example, we have produced scales of intercultural leadership competence for each dimension, and this is the basis of the IAP InterCultural Leadership Assessment Profiling instrument (see www.thtconsulting.com).

It is likely that the degree to which you reconcile is not the same for each cultural dimension. So consider those dimensions where your propensity to reconcile is lower. This model gives you a strategy to focus your attention on which dimensions you need to consider first to increase your effectiveness. If you can achieve this successfully, you are well on the way to a shared understanding with new business partners and a framework for developing your leadership competence.

Our research evidence from these instruments in our new reconciliation database confirms that intercultural competence, as defined by the propensity to reconcile dilemmas, correlates directly with 360-degree peer assessment of bottom-line business performance and is a key characteristic of effective leaders. Organizations that have such leaders with this competence at the individual level are effective at the corporate level in growing and surviving across the world in the global marketplace.

We can now follow this same logic through the process of globalization.

Universalistic vs. Particularistic Perspective

While we have often used dilemmas such as the car accident (which everyone can relate to), many equivalent real-world dilemmas have an impact on international managers. The most dominant and frequently occurring is the global–local dichotomy. This was clearly underlying the debate in our case in the beginning of this chapter. Shall we have one standardized approach as in the view of Mr. Daniels, Mr. Klaus and Ms. Jones, or shall we try the local, more particular approach? If we have a single universal model that appears to work in our own country, can we just replicate it around the globe? There are differing views on whether we are becoming more globally universal and alike or whether we are becoming more influenced by particular and unfamiliar national cultures.

In hindsight, this global local dilemma was one that very much jeopardized the success of the KLM–Alitalia alliance. The Protestant Dutch were sticklers for following the contract. The prepayment of some $100 million for the development of Malpensa Airport was one of the central conditions. The Italians saw it as a sign of the seriousness of the alliance rather than of the financial evaluation of the investment. When the investment failed to meet expectations, the Dutch began discussing prepayments: A contract is a contract. The Italians had all kinds of reasons why it was not going as planned. Life is hectic and might offer unexpected particular exceptions: "What's the problem? We'll do it in another way." But what a difference when Air France bought KLM. From the outset, the new French CEO Spinetta focused clearly on the things the new integrated company needed to share in order to allow as many differences as possible. The conclusion is very simple: We focus on IT, marketing/sales, purchasing and top management so that the brands, operations and crew can be unaffected. It can be called a successful integration, so much so that, a few years later, AlItalia was invited to become a member of the family. What can we learn from these types of successes and failures in the process of internationalization?

48   UNIVERSALISTIC/PARTICULARISTIC PERSPECTIVES

The bounding outcome behaviors in intercultural encounters can be identified as follows.

Ignore Other Cultures: The Global Corporation

One type of approach is to ignore the other orientation. You are sticking to your own (cultural) viewpoint. Your style of decision making is to impose your own way of doing things either because you believe that your way of doing things and your values are best or because you have rejected other ways of thinking or doing things because you do not recognize them or have no respect for them. Our aim is to help you to both recognize and respect cultural differences as the first step in reconciling differences. The Ford Mondeo (meaning "world car"), for example, was envisaged as a model to be both made and sold in an identical way across the world. Another great example in consulting is McKinsey, where local influences are minimized in their dominant approach. Even clients are frequently excluded when designing strategic interventions. It is "my way or the highway" at McKinsey. This is the global organization where HQ reigns and cultural diversity is ignored.

Abandon Your Own Orientation: The Multilocal Organization

The second type of response is to abandon HQ's orientation and go native wherever you can. Here the approach is, "When in Rome, do as the Romans do." Acting or keeping up such pretences won't go unnoticed; you will be very much an amateur. People from the other culture will mistrust you, and you won't be able offer your own strengths to any alliance. This has been the approach of the big four accountancy firms and for good reasons. The laws on financial transactions and tax were and are often local. These firms have great difficulty in globalizing, as we can see with KPMG and Deloitte.

Compromise: The International Organization

Sometimes do it your way. Sometimes give in to others. But this is a win/lose solution or even a lose/lose solution. Compromise cannot lead to a solution in which both parties are satisfied; something has to give. It leads to the international organization where most things are shared but with some local adaptations.

Some organizations were forced to do this because of the nature of their product or service. A good example is the Disney theme parks in Paris where they serve wine, in Japan where you can get sushi at lunch and in the U.S. where the burger and Coke dominate. It is the international organization with the Statue of Liberty holding a local flag.

Reconciliation: The Transnational Organization

In an increasingly more subtle and complex process of internationalization, these approaches show growing inefficiencies. What is needed is an approach where the two opposing views can fuse or blend—where the strength of one extreme is extended by considering and accommodating the other. This is reconciliation and is the approach that leads to your becoming more effective, especially in situations of diversity or working across cultures. One approach is to start from your own natural orientation but to accommodate the alternate viewpoint to achieve reconciliation. An alternative approach is to start from the opposite orientation to your normal values but then to embrace your own orientation and thus achieve the reconciliation you need.

Hence a company can adopt a global strategy in the extreme—by ignoring other cultures and replicating its original and successful universal approach across the world. It may run into problems, for example when trying to sell beef hamburgers in countries whose religion may forbid beef. Or it can adopt a multilocal approach, where it adapts to each particular location in which it is trading. But as a consequence, costs may rise because of the loss of economies of scale required to support different cultures. In addition, the organization may well lose its corporate identity or brand image.

At the corporate level, an organization needs to reconcile the single universalistic global approach with the multilocal particularistic approach. As we have demonstrated, compromise in a multinational company is not enough. What is needed is the reconciliation between the universal and the particular. In general, international success depends upon discovering special veins of excellence within different cultures. Just because people speak English does not mean they think alike. That no two cultures are the same is what brings richness and complexity to multinationalism. To achieve this reconciliation, an organization has to make a conceptual leap. The answer lies in transnational specialization, allowing each nation to specialize in what it does best and become a source of authority and leadership within the global corporation for that particular vein of excellence. The reach is truly global, but the sources of major influence are national. In particular, leadership functions shift to those nations that excel at those tasks. This cycle is in fact helical. (See Figure 4.2.)

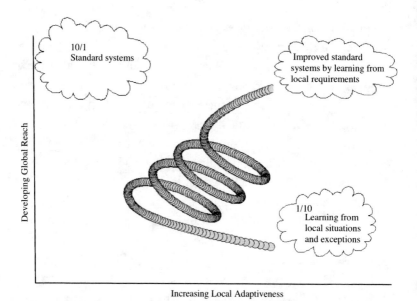

Figure 4.2 The Global–Local Tension and Its Reconciliation

Transnational organizations need to look for a similar logic: It is the result of incorporating particular learning efforts into a universal framework and vice versa. It is the connection between practical learning in a context of intelligent theories. Kurt Lewin sagely observed, "There is nothing more practical than a *good* theory." In this dialectic, the best integration processes are developed, and disadvantages are made into advantages. However, this effect is not easily achieved and needs the involvement of senior managers. This is known as the anticlockwise helix, meaning that you start at the horizontal (particular) axis and work your way to reconciliation by accommodating the vertical axis. (See Figure 4.3.)

When training managers across the globe, Heineken was faced with delivering their training program in the various countries in which they had a presence. But should they deliver one standard program in each destination (universal) or a different (particular)

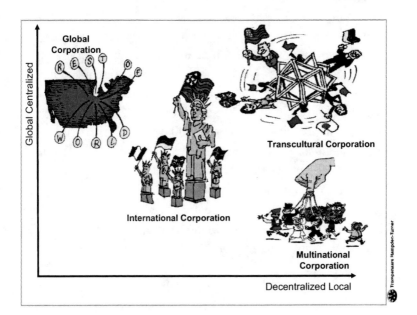

Figure 4.3 Learning from Best Practices

52 UNIVERSALISTIC/PARTICULARISTIC PERSPECTIVES

program to meet local needs? They successfully reconciled this dilemma by continuously approaching from both extremes. They used local knowledge as input to the design of a standard training program but then also adapted the improved generic program to meet local needs.

Even McDonald's, the icon of globalization and consistency, has started to develop transcultural traits. One of the most successful markets in the Western world has been France. Analyses showed that part of the success of McDonald's in France is the design of its restaurants. And what can be said about McDonald's when they invite the French interior designer to Manhattan to help refurnish all New York restaurants? Clearly this is an example of sharing best local practices and applying them globally!

In some situations, marketing strength derives from universal world branding. Thus Coca-Cola is Coca-Cola everywhere and represents the American dream, although the list of ingredients on the can or bottle may be in a local language. Similarly, Singapore Airlines exhibits the same "Asian" level of service to passengers of all nationalities, en route to the different destinations it serves.

There is an alternative to taking the best practices and globalizing them. When coauthor Trompenaars was asked to give a presentation for Applied Materials in Santa Clara, California, he was struck by the 57 nationalities in their top 100 employees. American CEO Jim Morgan shared power with his cofounder, who is Israeli. We met an Argentinean HR manager of Russian descent, a German head of technology and a French marketing VP. If what you deliver globally is developed by a multicultural team, the helix has become clockwise again. You start with a global approach that is sensitive to local circumstances because of the variety in your top team.

Implications for Performance Management

In cultures with a universalistic orientation, managers would be expected to appraise performance on how well the person or team performed the assigned duties and met the established goals. Ideally, the appraisal would not consider who the person or team was, the personal relationship with the manager or circumstances that were not job related. The factors that would be considered would be quality of work, productivity, dependability, adherence to policies/values, and the like. There would be a widespread use of predetermined goals, and actual results, measured against those standards, would be a major determinant of the appraisal rating.

In cultures with a particularistic orientation, managers would tend to consider personal relationships and the input provided by trusted acquaintances on the person's performance. Each person would be evaluated on their special merits, which would differ among individuals. Moreover, in particularistic environments, you'll find some consideration for the unique and special circumstances that the individual or group has been facing, which are taken into consideration for explaining higher or lower performance.

A reconciliation of the dilemma between a consistent application of rules (e.g., appraising all employees based on how well they did their jobs) and flexible application of rules based on relationships or circumstances (e.g., appraising the merits of the person) can be facilitated by establishing policies governing the factors used in performance appraisals. In addition to job-related results, other factors such as loyalty and contribution over time may be utilized in rating a person's performance. Extenuating circumstances should be considered as well, since employees should be held accountable only for those things they can control or influence. In cases where employees cannot control results, they typically can control their behavior, and if they exhibit appropriate behavior, this should be considered in the appraisal rating.

Even what the process of rating performance is called can make a difference. In the Middle East, the term "performance appraisal" is often taken to mean one person judging another. Coauthor Greene and a colleague have found that using the term "contribution review" to describe the process lessens this sensitivity.

A reconciliation is possible when the performance management philosophy incorporates the values of the organization, but freedom is given to the local operations as to how to apply them. Concurrently, HQ evaluates what is developed locally and continuously tests it to see whether it would work globally.

Implications for Rewards Management

If an organization bases rewards solely on performance against job standards, it can overlook valued contributions such as loyalty to the company, effort expended and possession of valuable tacit knowledge. A universalistic view of rewarding performance can result in everyone being treated the same, irrespective of their occupation and the nature of the work they perform. Activities such as mentoring and training less experienced peers may be overlooked, as well as the value of knowledge possessed by the person that is valuable to the functioning of the organization but not related to the person's current job and performance standards. Merit pay and individual incentive programs will generally be applied using established policies that generally preclude consideration of personal characteristics and relationships.

But if an organization bases rewards on factors other than performance standards and/or allows for personal characteristics and relationships to enter into the rewards allocation process, it opens the door to inconsistent application across managers. In some cases, this may result in charges of discrimination, particularly in countries such as the U.S. that have laws mandating that rewards be tied to individual job-related results and behaviors. In order for an organization to meet its objectives, it is necessary to align the efforts of all employees, and a particularistic approach to rewards may result in a dissipated focus. If some employees are rewarded based on relationships, other employees will view this as unfair, and the organization may not get the results it intended to pay for.

A reconciliation of the dilemma between universalistic and particularistic approaches to allocating rewards can be facilitated by ensuring that rewards reflect contributions to organizational success, however defined. Employees who make others more effective by sharing their knowledge and exhibiting supportive behavior should be rewarded for those contributions. If extenuating circumstances make it more difficult for some individuals to achieve their objectives, this should be considered in reward allocation. Incentive plans that are based on aggregate performance can minimize a singular focus on individual performance measured in quantitative metrics and can encourage all employees to contribute everything they can.

Note

1. S. A. Stouffer and J. Toby, "Role Conflict and Personality," *American Journal of Sociology*, LUI-5 (1951): 395–406.

5
RECONCILING INDIVIDUALISTIC WITH COLLECTIVIST PERSPECTIVES

Back to Qwenchy. Ms. Jones was trying to summarize the variety of viewpoints and said that she was quite worried about the mix of views, varying from a belief in a consistent and standardized approach, favored by Klaus and her, to a preference for some flexibility, favored by most of the others. What to do? In a flash, it came to her. "Why," asked Ms. Jones, "don't we try first look at the existing processes we are applying in the variety of countries, take the best aspects of each of them and combine them in a way that creates a 'next practice' rather than just the 'best practice'?"

"Why," added Mr. Khasmi, "don't we take the suggested values of Mr. Daniels as a point of departure and apply performance and reward structures that work at the various locations and also support the values of our point of departure?"

"That's fine," said Mr. Mantovani, "but we in Italy would like to discuss some of those values and the Ten Principles, which are not seen as very wise in Milano."

"Mr. Mantovani, I fully agree with you," added Mr. Yakomoto. "There are many assumptions in the Ten Principles offered by

Mr. Daniels. Let's take the first, where he suggests that the system should focus on appraising specific results of the *individual* as output, and *individual* function-specific behavior as input. We will have a lot of problems with that in Japan."

"Wait a second," interjected Ms. Jones. "It's individuals who can perform and behave—teams cannot. That's why we chose this approach."

Mr. Klaus nodded his head to show agreement. Klaus is very happy with the introduction of an individualized pay-for-performance system; this can be a very strong motivational force. And he also added that the final responsibility should remain in the hands of the individual; otherwise, too many individuals will run the risk of hiding behind the backs of the others. "What we need at Qwenchy are entrepreneurs who take their own initiative and take their own responsibility."

Mr. Yakomoto was taken aback but continued his line of thought and added: "Furthermore, I believe it is a shared responsibility of both superior and manager to improve performance. Evaluating performance is not sufficient. The appraiser should not act only as a judge. It is his or her responsibility to support and lead the appraisee to even better performances by practicing mentorship, making development/training plans and so on. Therefore, I find it necessary that the system stresses this."

Mr. Khasmi agreed. "I do not believe in the principles of individual pay-for-performance as favored by Daniels. I believe it is unfair to reward individuals at the cost of the team. Mr. Yakomoto and I think it is more motivating to reward a group (a department or division) than individual persons. If the group is motivated to work hard and receives a salary increase, every single individual will benefit from that. But it doesn't work the other way around. On the contrary, if an individual is rewarded extra for outstanding results, it might even demotivate the group. (Why are we all working so hard if we are not allowed to share in the profit?) Hence, the competitive aspect of individual

INDIVIDUALISTIC/COLLECTIVIST PERSPECTIVES 59

pay-for-performance can have a disruptive aspect on the functioning of a team."

The meeting became very quiet.

Individualistic vs. Collectivist Perspectives

The dimension of culture at issue in this conversation deals with an orientation to the individual or the collective. Do we relate to others by discovering what each of us individually wants and then trying to negotiate the differences or by emphasizing concern for the public and collective good?

People with an *individualistic* orientation believe they should have as much freedom as possible and the maximum opportunity to develop themselves. There is a prime orientation to the self. Country cultures that tend to be individualistic include those in the Western and Northern parts of the world.

Those with a *collectivist* orientation believe that people should take care of others and the group/organization, even if it obstructs individual freedom and individual development. They have a strong orientation to common goals and objectives. Countries that tend to be collectivist include Middle Eastern, Latin and Asian countries.

The difference between individual and group orientations is about how we resolve the conflict between our individual interests and objectives and those of the group to which we belong:

- Do we relate to others by determining what each one of us wants and then negotiating the differences? (Individualism)
- Or do we relate to them by giving priority to a shared idea of what is good for the group? (Collectivism)

Again, cultures differ in which orientation they primarily focus on, as can be shown by the following dilemma:

Two people were discussing ways in which individuals could improve the quality of life.

a) One said: "It is obvious that if individuals have as much freedom as possible and the maximum opportunity to develop themselves, the quality of their life will improve as a result."

b) The other said: "If individuals are continuously taking care of their fellow human beings, the quality of life will improve for everyone, even if it obstructs individual freedom and individual development."

Which of the two ways of reasoning do you think is usually best—a or b?

The percentages of respondents who think that the quality of life improves with giving freedom to the individual are shown in Figure 5.1.

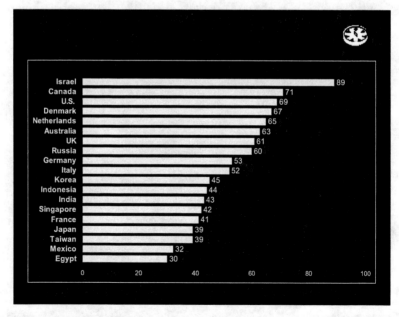

Figure 5.1 Percentage Opting for Individual Freedom—Individual vs. Group Orientation (How to Improve the Quality of Life)

INDIVIDUALISTIC/COLLECTIVIST PERSPECTIVES 61

Some Key Findings

- Israelis score highest on this indicator of individual orientation (89% opting for individual freedom).
- Also scoring high are Canadians, Americans and Danes, of whom more than 65% favor individual freedom.
- Among the French, 41% opt for individual freedom,
- In many Asian countries, including Singapore, Japan and India, only about 40% or less opt for individual freedom.

Individualism is often regarded as characteristic of a modern society, and group orientation, in contrast, is reminiscent of more traditional societies and the failed communist experiment. However, the success of the so-called Five Dragons (Japan, Hong Kong, Singapore, South Korea and Taiwan) raises questions as to whether it is the only and thus inevitable way toward modernization and affluence. China increasingly challenges the notion that only one cultural orientation can lead to economic growth.

Table 5.1 Implications of Individual vs. Group Orientation for Rewards

Assumption underlying rewards that link pay and promotion to performance	Potential obstacles to rewarding individual performance in group-oriented cultures:
1. Individuals seek to be distinguished from the rest of the group.	Certain individuals feel neglected because the winner takes it all.
2. Singling out individuals for praise is OK with their colleagues.	Can be seen as threat to team spirit; creates competition, not cooperation.
3. An individual's contribution to a common task can easily be identified	It is difficult to motivate people to share their knowledge and coordinate their efforts.
4. Motivation occurs only when rewards are based on individual results.	Supervisors may attempt to rate everyone similarly to avoid conflict, distorting the actual performance of individuals.
5. The unit and the organization will benefit only if individuals perform.	The efforts of individuals may result in each performing well, but if those efforts are not aligned, the overall goals may not be met.

INDIVIDUALISTIC/COLLECTIVIST PERSPECTIVES

Representation and Status

Group-oriented cultures prefer plural representation. There are reasons why plural representation is preferred by some of the meeting participants. They feel it is necessary to represent the microcosms of interests existing in their countries and Qwenchy subsidiaries. They are there at the meeting as delegates, bound by the wishes of those who sent them. And this has an impact on how they believe decisions should be made.

Decision Making in Group-Oriented Cultures

- Typically, decision making takes much longer than in individualistic societies.
- Sustained efforts are made to engage everybody in achieving consensus.
- Usually, detailed consultations occur with all those concerned.
- The many minor objections raised are typically practical rather than personal or principled.
- The consensus may be modified in many respects.
- There is pressure to agree on collective goals, which usually leads to consensus.
- If the group or home office is not consulted first, an initial yes may turn into a no later.
- Voting down the dissenters is unacceptable: It lacks respect for those who are against the majority decision.
- The final result takes longer to achieve but will be much more stable.
- Because those consulted will usually have to implement the consensus, the implementation phase proceeds smoothly and easily.

Decision Making in Individual-Oriented Cultures

- Respect for individual opinions is strong.
- Frequent voting occurs.
- Those who are in the minority accept the vote.
- Those outvoted have another chance at the next vote.
- The process of arriving at a decision is fast.

- People may revert to their original opinion after the vote.
- There is a potential disparity between decision and implementation.

Decision Making Assessed Across Cultures

Consider a second question measuring individual and group orientation:

In your experience, when a decision has to be made, people will look for:
a) a compromise, as this will save precious time. All the people involved need to vote.
b) a consensus, even if it takes more time. All the people involved need to accept the outcome.

In this second example, the individualist viewpoint is reflected in the percentage of decisions made by voting for a compromise. (See Figure 5.2.)

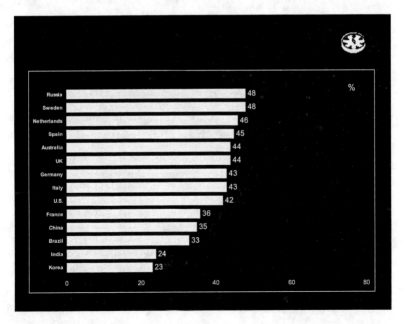

Figure 5.2 Individual vs. Group Orientation—Percentage of Respondents Who Think Decisions Should Be Made by Compromising

64 INDIVIDUALISTIC/COLLECTIVIST PERSPECTIVES

Recognition

In addition to differences in how decisions are made, linguistic differences also enable one to recognize individualistic or communitarian cultures. For example, in individualistic cultures, " I" is written with a capital letter. In many languages, you write "I" with a lowercase letter and "you" with a capital letter. And what about introducing oneself ? In individualistic societies like the U.S., you introduce yourself by first and last name but suggest you be called by your first name. In many communitarian societies, it is the reverse.

Implications for Performance Management

Performance can be defined and measured at the individual, the group or the organization-wide level. Using performance appraisals to evaluate the performance of individual employees can produce a focus on getting one's job done and meeting one's assigned objectives, irrespective of how well the group/unit/organization does. Tying rewards for the individual (money, career advancement, prestige, desirable work assignments) to how well the person performs motivates that employee to focus on his or her own work.

Defining and measuring performance at an aggregate level can produce a focus on each individual doing whatever is necessary to produce the desired results at the aggregate level. When rewards are based on aggregate performance, everyone in the collective receives the same or a proportionate share of the available rewards. The motivation for the individual is to contribute to the effectiveness of other group members and to consider how his or her own work contributes to the desired aggregate result.

A reconciliation of the dilemma between an individualistic definition of performance and a collectivist definition can be facilitated by incorporating factors into individual performance appraisals that measure the degree to which the person contributed to the effectiveness of peers and to the success of the unit, in addition to how well the individual carried out his or her responsibilities and whether goals were met. For example, a rating factor such as "Contribution to the effectiveness of others" and/or "Contribution to the effectiveness of the unit" can be added to the productivity, quality of work and dependability/adherence to rules that are typically used to rate support employees. And when evaluating management and professional employees, the contribution factors can be built into the responsibilities and the performance objectives that are typically used to rate performance for these employees.

Not including the importance of doing one's work in a manner that contributes to the effectiveness of others and the unit/organization allows an individualistic employee to ignore this critical aspect of performance. On the other hand, collectivist employees must understand that they must play their part in overall success by developing their competence and putting forth their best efforts. For example, in a research team that includes professionals with advanced knowledge in a variety of disciplines, a focus on both individual and team performance is required: The physicist must do the physics in the best way possible but also consider how her work fits into the multidisciplinary work of the team.

Implications for Rewards Management

A widely accepted premise is, "What you measure and reward, you will most surely get more of."

If an organization defines, measures and rewards performance at the individual level alone, it can produce a singular focus on personal achievement. Reward programs such as merit pay and individual incentive plans define performance at the individual level and reward individual results. This approach will tend to motivate employees to perform their work well. But if the funds available for merit increases or individual incentives are fixed in amount, it may produce competitive behavior. So if the nature of the work requires cooperative behavior, a group of employees may perform at high levels individually but result in poor performance at the aggregate

66 INDIVIDUALISTIC/COLLECTIVIST PERSPECTIVES

level. It should not be a surprise that a world-class sports team will typically defeat an all-star team. In the U.S., the NBA all-star game puts five people on a team, but each will typically be used to handling the ball 30–40% of the time—a mathematical impossibility in all-star play. As a result, the game often turns into a series of individual efforts that do not result in selfless actions such as assists, setting screens and the like. There is, of course, intense competition to be the Player of the Game, and this honor is accompanied by financial rewards.

If an organization defines, measures and rewards performance at the aggregate (group, unit, organization-wide) level it will tend to focus individuals on doing their work in a manner that produces the best overall results, with a diminished focus on individual results. Reward programs such as profit sharing and group/team/organization-wide incentive plans will motivate employees to focus more on overall results and less on how individual performance compares to that of other employees. However, if the funds available for rewards are distributed in an egalitarian manner, it opens the door to "social loafing" by individuals who may believe their lack of contribution may not be noticed and that others will take up the slack.

A reconciliation of the dilemma between rewarding at the individual level or the aggregate level is to reward performance at all levels (individual *and* team *and* organizational rather than individual *or* team *or* organizational). Given a combination of individual rewards programs and group/unit/organization-wide rewards programs, each employee is motivated to perform at high levels at the individual level and to do so in a manner that contributes to the performance of peers, the unit and the organization. A profit-sharing plan may act as a "shared destiny" plan, rewarding all individuals for producing the desired results at an organizational level. Group incentive plans may focus employees on the performance of their unit (team, department, function, business unit). Merit pay plans may motivate high levels of individual performance. By combining all three, an organization can convey the message to employees that performance will be defined, measured and rewarded at all levels.

An example will make the point even clearer.

Co-Opetition: Compete for the Best Cooperation

In the early 2000s, we see an increasing number of companies opting for more variable pay. Philips, the Dutch electronics giant, even considered breaking their important Collective Labour Agreement to be able to do so in the year 2000. The fight between fixed income and variable income is always a tough one, since many employees will opt for a certain pay level and resent risking some of that based on results. And appraisal and rewards systems have attracted lots of attention in the management literature of the last century. The overarching question is how can people be motivated and the best people retained? And how can management effectively provide feedback to employees on their performance? It is striking how many research findings have indicated that money is not motivating under certain circumstances. Maslow's hierarchy of needs model tells us that if people are worried about job security or feel their jobs are unchallenging and if they do not utilize their skills, these issues may become more important than money (assuming they are paid enough to meet their subsistence and security needs). And employees quickly get over the good feelings associated with a pay adjustment or bonus. When a financial reward is below expectations, it can have a significant impact on motivation and satisfaction.

Money, however, can play a very positive role, as a symbol for much deeper values. The relative feeling of having earned more than a colleague seems to be much more important than the absolute pecuniary value of the bonus. On the extreme end of the scale, we have the front-runners of the so-called New Economy in which financial consultants and e-commerce staff had 60–90% variable pay. If you then analyze the relationship between the quality of their functioning with the growth of turnover and profitability, the question needs to be raised how large their contribution actually is. Just have a look at Nina Brink of World Online, who became billionaire with a very mediocre business concept. Even with appallingly bad management, one can raise enormous income. A classic research study from Northwestern University showed that only 10% of the results of an organization is directly in the control of management. So big rewards for something that would have happened anyway seem out of line, particularly to someone with a collectivist orientation.

The financial crisis of 2007–2012 can be at least partially attributed to incentive award schemes that made people wealthy even though their work resulted in disaster for their organizations and the banking world. And executive incentives that motivated management into misstating financial results to keep the annual rewards coming have been the subject of scrutiny by regulatory agencies and national legislatures.

Coauthor Trompenaars met an American HR manager who claimed that his company had developed a very interesting pay-for-performance scheme. Total rewards were at least 50% in the form of variable pay, including attractive share options that would materialize after only three years of active service. Short- and long-term thinking was reconciled in this approach, and people seem to be highly motivated because they believed they had a direct effect on the functioning of the organization as a whole. He had to admit, however, that this approach was less readily accepted in both Europe and Asia. In Europe, the reason seemed to be mainly fiscal constraints, but in Asia the reason was quite unclear. "Could it be culture?" he asked. The solution is quite straightforward. In Asia, you can motivate people by a team reward structure. In Europe, it really doesn't matter as long as you can avoid taxes. But there is a hidden problem. This decentralized approach works very well when you are part of a multinational organization. If, however, you

INDIVIDUALISTIC/COLLECTIVIST PERSPECTIVES 69

grow into a transnational firm, characterized by many multicultural teams, in which many motivational systems are united, the reward system needs to be adapted accordingly.

The internationalization process forces us to adapt much of the existing logic in management thinking. There are some options that do not work as well. The first one is to train every employee to be able to take the responsibility for his or her own creativity. On the collective level, this is called the *individualization of society*. But this can create a problem because the individualized human being is not keen on sharing information. You can also choose a reward stimulating team spirit. People from Japan excel at this, but it often leads to collective mediocrity. The worst is the compromise, that is, rewarding the small team. Both the individualist and the team player feel demotivated. So what is the alternative?

Consider the developments of rewards in the U.S. semiconductor industry. Isn't it amazing that, due to the Asian effectiveness in the 1980s, a complete industry was on the edge of being wiped out, after which it has made an unprecedented comeback, partly due to agreements made in the cooperative institution of Sematech? The American Ministry of Defense founded Sematech to enable American chip manufacturers to have their suppliers cooperate to better compete with their Asian competition—a classic example of *co-opetition*: cooperate to compete.

You could also find this spirit in the organizations themselves, such as in Intel, AMD and National Semiconductor. Their reward schemes are all aimed at having creative individualists molding teams that achieve beyond expectations. They managed to do so and see the result. At the end of the 1980s, Shell tried an experiment in the north of Amsterdam with 2,000 staff in the R&D division called KSLA. Shell tried to stimulate creative individualistic researchers to create effective multicultural teamwork. Annually, the variable pay awards were evenly distributed between individual and team bonuses. The individual bonus was given to the individual that was chosen by the team as the best team player. The team bonus was given to the team that excelled in supporting individual creativity. The Shell researchers from Amsterdam competed for the best cooperation in teams, and they cooperated to be better able to compete.

Another recent example was advice a consultant gave to IBM's sales force. Instead of giving a bonus to those who sold the most, he advised an alternative reward strategy. Every quarter, the salespersons had to make presentations of what they had learned from their customers in the last period. And the audience consisted of colleagues. Sales went up by 30%, client satisfaction improved and information was exchanged among colleagues, while taking advantage of the existing competitive spirit. This is another example of co-opetition: competing for the cooperation with the client. The best sales staff, we learned later, also learned the most from the client.

Back to Qwenchy. Ms. Jones was getting increasingly worried about all these differing viewpoints. Wouldn't it be easier if everyone would just follow the approach put forward by Mr. Daniels? "All this nonsense about groups and their behaviors," she was thinking. "I really think they're trying to walk away from their responsibilities."

Mr. Klaus got a bit irritated and said that if we would just go all global and follow the HQ's guidelines, all would be fine.

Mr. Mantovani from Italy waved with his hands while saying: "I would be very unhappy with individual pay for performance. Although I believe that pay for performance can indeed be a very strong motivational tool, I don't like the idea that it focuses on the individual. In my view, it works against teamwork. Imagine person A gets a salary increase because she has reached all the fixed targets. And assume that this person could reach the targets only thanks to the continuous help and input of person B (who for other justifiable reasons could not reach his targets). It would be utterly unfair to reward person A and not person B. This kind of rewarding can eventually have a very negative impact on the business because, possibly, the next time person B will think twice before helping and supporting person A! As an alternative, I would like to propose that rewards are based on departmental/divisional performance. A bonus for high performance (that is, reaching the divisional targets) will then be equally distributed amongst all employees in the department/division." Mr. Mantovani was obviously irritated and suggested in a side conversation that his teams would be motivated by different things, so why not have everyone do their own thing?

Mr. Khasmi asked for the microphone and presented his experience in Dubai. "Ladies and gentlemen. In our research center in the UAE we had the applied researchers asking for more group attention, since they were so dependent on one another. The fundamental researchers, however, felt they were so good individually that they wanted an individual bonus. What we did is to base 50% of the bonus on the individual and 50% on team performance. Unfortunately, it didn't work because the fundamental researchers were still not inclined to work with the applied researchers; they just focused on the 50% individual rewards. It was a compromise. But when we added the stipulation that individuals could get a bonus only when they shared their ideas with the applied teams and that the teams could get a bonus when they looked after the creativity of the individual researcher, it started to become effective. It took us three years, however." All nodded in agreement that this would also work in their environment.

The dialogue continued among group members. "And on top of all the problems we have identified, I think that this proposed system is so clinical, so controlled, so detached," started Mr. Mantovani. "How do we stimulate passion in people? . . . This looks so calculated. If we want more entrepreneurs, we need more passion in our system. That is what makes them successful. Also, I have numerous comments to make on the so-called Ten Principles. If Italian employees were to read them, they would burst into laughter . . . or react in anger. We are an emotionally expressive people, and I pray to the lord that I will not lose my temper during these meetings!"

Ms. Jones and Mr. Klaus looked at each other in amazement. How can he say that? Their common expression said, without a word being spoken, "The Italians are nuts!" One of the most important reasons for introducing this system is to be more objective and detached. Even entrepreneurs need to control their emotions and become objective.

Ms. Jones emphasized that judgments must be made based on performance and business results and that they should not let themselves be misled by any kind of personal and emotional preference. Managers should not be biased by prejudices and should leave the "person" out of consideration. Moreover, the Ten Principles of Mr. Daniels state that we need not let strong or weak points of the appraisee influence our evaluation of other criteria. And we should not be influenced by the previous performance of the appraisee; a past success or blunder should not bias the appraisal for the current period. Finally, judgments should be based on concrete facts: not on notions or assumptions. The appraisal must be as objective as possible.

6
RECONCILING NEUTRAL WITH AFFECTIVE PERSPECTIVES

In our relationships with others, reason and emotion both play roles. How we see the relationships between the two depends on whether we have a controlled orientation toward emotions or an expressive orientation. The difference between the two orientations lies not in how strongly people feel about something but in cultural conventions related to revealing emotions. Members of control-oriented cultures see emotions as independent of reason and believe that emotions tend to get in the way of a rational, objective approach to a situation. They also tend to believe they should control their emotions and keep them subdued. Members of expressive-oriented cultures see emotions as an integral part of who they are and how they think about an issue, and they show their feelings openly—laughing, smiling, grimacing, scowling and gesturing while communicating with others. Finally, they try to find immediate outlets for their feelings.

How Is the Difference in Emotional Expression Across Cultures Assessed?

Participants in THT research were asked what they do when they feel upset about something at work: Would they express their feelings openly?

73

What do you think of the following statement? (1=strongly agree, 5=strongly disagree)
In cases where one feels upset at work, one is inclined to express it.

Some Key Findings (see also Figure 6.1)

- Cultures differ as to whether emotions can be expressed openly at work.
- Showing emotion is the least acceptable in Japan (74% of respondents said they would not show emotions openly).
- It is somewhat more acceptable in India and Singapore.
- Within Europe, there are considerable differences.
- Sweden is the most control oriented.
- Latin Europe and the Middle East are the least control oriented.
- There does not seem to be a general pattern by continent.

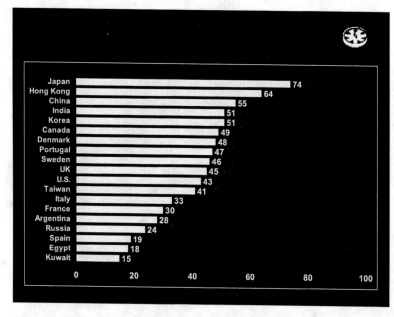

Figure 6.1 Controlled vs. Expressive—Would You Show Your Emotions Overtly?: Percentage of Respondents Who Would Not Show Their Emotions Overtly at Work

NEUTRAL/AFFECTIVE PERSPECTIVES

What Are the Implications of the Difference Between Controlled and Expressive Orientation for Doing Business?

There is a significant potential for misunderstanding.

Control-Oriented Cultures

- People may come across as cold and unfeeling.
- People may be viewed as emotionally constipated or repressed.
- People may appear to be uninvolved and disinterested.
- People may be seen as too formal and thus untrustworthy.

Expression-Oriented Cultures

- People may come across as uncontrolled.
- People may appear not to be businesslike and viewed as unprofessional.
- The emotional involvement shown may be felt to be overwhelming: "I'd better watch out. He looks like he is going to jump at me."
- People's emotions may be magnified for effect.

Beware of Humor, Understatement and Irony

Cultures also differ in their appreciation of humor. In workshops in Britain and the U.S., we often start with a cartoon or anecdote to lighten up the discussion of the points to be covered. This always goes down well. Hence Fons kicked off a THT workshop in Germany, with some confidence, with a cartoon deriding European differences. Nobody laughed; instead, people took notes. But as the week went by, there was a lot of laughter at the bar and eventually also during the sessions. People simply had not expected humor in a professional setting between strangers.

A British audience may be underwhelmed by, say, irony at a presentation or regard it with subdued rapture—a device to control emotional expression by triggering emotional release in the form of

76 NEUTRAL/AFFECTIVE PERSPECTIVES

laughter. This way you can have it both ways! A Japanese superior will similarly rebuke an incompetent subordinate by exaggerated deference. "If you could see your way to kindly troubling yourself in a matter so minor, I would be in your debt." In expressive language, this translates as, "Do it or else."

One of the common justifications for events in the movie *The Godfather* was, "This isn't personal; it's business." Even though the characters were of Italian descent, they were in America and acting from a neutral perspective.

Implications for Performance Management

When performance is defined and measured objectively, we can start with the assignment of objectives and responsibilities to individual people. This works very well in neutral cultures where no emotion should stand in the way of this very rational process. Performance in neutral cultures often allows for a multisource input by a 360-degree process. And if we find agreement, neutral objectivity has been achieved.

Managers in neutral cultures are expected to "tell it like it is" and are viewed as deceitful and not acting like good managers if they do not. The focus is expected to be on job-related results and behaviors and on nothing else, no matter who the person is. Effort that produces no results may also be ignored, although someone who continuously puts forth his or her best effort may be given the chance to improve. Managers may be expected to identify appropriate training or to provide guidance to improve competence. But all should be communicated fully and directly.

In more affective cultures, where emotions are readily available and expressed, performance appraisal gets much more emotional. It is the courage with which one tries things that counts, even if the actual objective is not completely met. And even liking the person, the team and their efforts is at least as important as the final results. However, when personal feelings impact appraisal ratings, there

NEUTRAL/AFFECTIVE PERSPECTIVES

may be negative implications if laws and case precedents dictate that only job-related results and behaviors are legitimate factors for evaluating and rewarding performance.

A reconciliation of the dilemma between a neutral and controlled definition of performance and an expressive and affective definition can be facilitated by incorporating factors into objective performance appraisals that measure the degree to which the person contributed to the level of passion with which the goals were achieved, contributing to the success of the final outcome.

Implications for Rewards Management

Rewards are significantly impacted by whether you are operating in a controlled or expressive environment.

In a controlled environment, the criteria for determining rewards are objectively set at the beginning, and no negotiation is possible around it. It is very often limited to financial measures that at least communicate objectivity and focus. In some cases, a U.S. manager may give a friend a poor rating and then make up for it by treating the friend to an expensive dinner, which partially makes up for the smaller pay increase the poor rating will result in. Because that reward comes out of the manager's pocket rather than the company's, the policies don't apply.

Reward systems in affective and expressive cultures tend to be more focused on subjective and emotional factors like the thrill of being promoted or recognition for a good effort, even if it did not lead to success. Also the total amount of the rewards might be increased or decreased at the last moment involving the latest emotions.

A reconciliation of the rewards dilemma is indicated in research findings. One can receive a neutral reward like a bonus and also experience an emotional reward if the bonus is accompanied by praise for doing a great job: The bonus becomes a symbol of success. Conversely, when an emotional response to a promotion

Controlled Points of View Reconciled with Expressed Ones

Back to Qwenchy. Mr. Mantovani was pleased that most people in the meeting understood his call for passion. Isn't that what makes up an entrepreneur? Ms. Jones summarized it so nicely: "If we can continually supplement our intuition and emotions with concrete outcomes, we will develop a program that works in all countries."

Ms. Jones liked the idea of separating the person from the task. According to her, this is the only way to ensure objectivity and fair play. Staff appraisals and performance and reward management should definitely focus on achieving specific results.

Mr. Khasmi reacts to this assumption by claiming that he fears that many of the Ten Principles are not applicable in the UAE due to cultural constraints (e.g., the issue of separating the task from the person and being frank, open and confrontational, both of which can lead to the appraisee's losing face).

Mr. Mantovani nods his head and agrees fully with his Arab colleague: "As we discuss this more, I am not very happy with the outline proposed by Daniels. The Ten Principles run counter to too many of our cultural values, and I believe the outline for the system based on these would be an ethnocentric one, making only the Americans happy. Actually, the memo of Daniels has quite upset me. In my humble opinion, Daniels' view of staff appraisal is an act of judging instead of coaching. Everything is about measuring and judging 'specific results,' isolated from the person. Is that Daniels' definition of an employee? A machine to produce results? Did he forget that employees are humans? There is more to work than only business results. How can you appraise somebody without taking the whole person into account?"

NEUTRAL/AFFECTIVE PERSPECTIVES

"No," says Mr. Klaus. "I am very happy and support any proposal with a task/result focus. I would like to place the emphasis on objectivity. You know that staff appraisal meetings are easily prone to be personally biased, and I want to avoid that at any cost. I think it is an excellent idea to include the Ten Principles, in particular where Daniels indicates that the system should focus on appraising specific results as output and function-specific behavior as input. And I support his contention that you need to evaluate each appraisal criterion in isolation. Do not let strong or weak points of the appraisee influence your evaluation of other criteria. And finally he states correctly that judgments need to be based on concrete facts, not on notions or assumptions. The appraisal must be as objective as possible. And I also concur with Mr. Daniels when he says we need to be honest, open, frank and direct and not wary of confrontations."

"Thank you, Mr. Klaus, for the open and frank reaction," continues Mr. Yakomoto, "but in my humble opinion, too much emphasis is usually placed on the task aspects of the job. It seems that the human dimension is often underappreciated. I would like to appraise people not only on the basis of what and how much they achieved but also on the basis of how they achieved it (with creativity, by successfully working in teams and so on). Quality and integrity are just as important as output. As far as competencies are concerned, I believe that far more emphasis should be placed on leadership skills and on the ability to coach and develop others, particularly if the person is a manager. If a person is excellent at achieving business results but hopeless in developing teamwork, coaching and leadership skills, that employee has done only part of the job. You find it important that staff appraisal is not seen as an isolated thing, a boring form that has to be filled out once a year, supposedly as an integrated part of total management. Therefore, the system should stress both task management and people management. Just as you have to deal with an employee as a total person, you must appraise him or her on total management skills. And, finally, I am opposed

NEUTRAL/AFFECTIVE PERSPECTIVES

to the idea of pay for performance. If you have to stimulate and motivate your employees with financial incentives, there must be something wrong with your management style. The organization should create an atmosphere in which people are proud and happy to work for their company.

"Thank you, gentlemen, for your feedback," says Ms. Jones. "*What a mess!*" she thinks to herself.

7
RECONCILING SPECIFIC WITH DIFFUSE PERSPECTIVES

This dimension of culture deals with how different cultures define what is public and what is private and thus the degree of involvement in relationships. Those with a specific orientation tend to see themselves as people who segregate their task or business relationships from personal relationships. This may be expressed in the value you attach to being direct, open and extroverted, as well as in giving your work life priority over your private life. Taking specificity to the extreme might lead to a lack of true personal involvement. People with a specific orientation tend to initially see people with a more diffuse orientation as indirect, reserved and evasive and find it hard to make initial contact with them.

More diffuse people might consider themselves to be modest, initially reserved with new relationships, but in the end they tend to be warm and much more personally involved in the business relationship. In their eyes, specific cultures may appear to be superficial and blunt, and your directness might make people with a diffuse orientation "lose face."

Closely related to whether we show emotions in dealing with other people is the degree to which we engage others in specific areas of life and single levels of personality, or diffusely in multiple areas of our lives and at several levels of personality at the same time.

SPECIFIC/DIFFUSE PERSPECTIVES

In specific-oriented cultures a manager segregates her task relationship with a subordinate and isolates this from other dealings. But in some countries, every life space and every level of personality tend to permeate all others.

An example might help. Someone asks you whether you're married, and you say, "Yes." They then ask, "What for?" If your response is, "Predominantly to gain a tax deduction," then that's a specific type of cultural response. If you say, "I don't know; it's love," then that's a diffuse cultural response. And obviously the reconciliation is whether you love tax deductions. Now, a specific culture involves people who believe in shareholder value—value created for people who never share. A diffuse culture is a culture where it's all about *Ganzheitlichkeit, Weltanschauung*; it's diffuse, and it is holistic. A specific approach is analytic. Kurt Lewin, a famous German psychologist, said, "Americans are amazing people. They are very open. You hardly know them and they talk to you. How can the Americans be so open?" The Americans can be so open because they have private things they keep to themselves. This is like a peach—easy to enter but then you hit the pit.

What is public in America? When Trompenaars was in America, a friend helped him move. At the end of the day, both were tired, and Fons said: "Bill, do you like a beer?" He turned around, and he was already in my refrigerator. For an American, a refrigerator is public; for most Europeans, it's closed—"Don't go into my refrigerator."

For the first three months, I didn't have a car. In typical American fashion, friends offered their cars. Have you tried it in Germany? Take my Mercedes—are you kidding? Take my kids but leave my Mercedes. If you are in America, very often you see people move, and they leave their furniture because furniture is public. In France it's considered antique. You can't get rid of it. It belongs to the family. Trompenaars's house is full of this old rubbish, but it belongs to the family, so we don't sell it.

SPECIFIC/DIFFUSE PERSPECTIVES

83

Kurt Lewin called the specific relationship the U-type (U.S.). He was a German, so the diffuse orientation is the G-type. In America, they will give you a title—Dr. Greene or Dr. Trompenaars—but they use it only in the university. You go one step outside of the university, people say, "Hello, Fons" or "Hello, Bob." In Austria, you are "Herr Doktor" everywhere—at work, in academia, or at the local store.

In a diffuse relationship, you are "Herr Doktor," and your wife is called "Frau Doktor." "Herr Doktor" is not a specific public label; "Herr Doktor" is you! It defines your identity. But "Dr. Greene" is "Bob" in America just about everywhere, except with students who feel that using the "Dr. Greene" form of address might have a positive impact on their grades.

Consider a meeting between Marketing and Research & Development. The R&D team has presented an idea to the marketing team, and the marketing people say, "It's a lousy idea."

What does that mean in the minds of the R&D people? Because R&D is a diffuse culture, the idea represents them, who they are. They don't separate the idea from their self-identity. So the marketing team has just offended the R&D team. The marketing team would not see it that way because they are very open, and it's impossible to insult them. You can say anything about them because they don't take it personally, which is evidence of a specific culture. What's happened here is that the marketers have strayed into the "danger zone" of privacy by inadvertently moving into the private arena of the R&D team. For the marketing team, discussing ideas is a public matter. For the R&D team, it's private. (See Figure 7.1.)

This is where the concept of "losing face" arises. Losing face is making public what is perceived as being private. And we all know how important it is to maintain face in countries like Japan and Spain. This is the big problem between cultures. It's where a diffuse culture meets a specific culture. A diffuse culture is recognized by

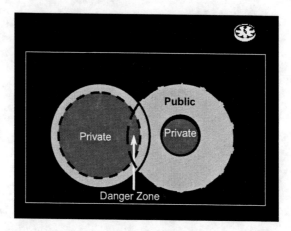

Figure 7.1 The Danger Zone Between What's Public and What's Private

indirect communication. There's a big difference between the British and the Americans. The Americans go straight to the point like the Dutch and the Australians. The English and the Japanese go indirectly. If they think something is wrong, they say, "It's a very interesting presentation that needs more research." The Dutch would say, "It is junk."

In Trompenaars's *The Seven Cultures of Capitalism*, the chapter on the Dutch is called: "You're an Idiot But Don't Take It Personally."

Losing Face: Encounters Between Specific and Diffuse

A final example of reconciliation is seen in the answer to the question that we ask people to find out whether they are more specific or diffuse. The boss asks you to paint his house. There are two arguments: "I don't have to paint his house." That's obviously specific—that's not part of the relationship. Or, "Yes, it's my boss, I have to do it," which is diffuse.

People with a Specific Orientation

- Have large public circles—many topics are in the public domain.

SPECIFIC/DIFFUSE PERSPECTIVES 85

- Can easily be frank and direct.
- May not fully understand how much a diffuse-oriented person considers private.

People with a Diffuse Orientation

- Have large private circles—criticism of their work is easily seen as criticism of them as persons.
- May often feel provoked by specific-oriented people.
- Spend a lot of time to get to the point in order to avoid loss of face.

Dress Code: Differences by Orientation

- Diffuse cultures: People tend to dress in the same style at work and in their private lives.
- Specific cultures: People tend to dress for the occasion.

Let us test the understanding of this dimension with a case that we have come across in our work. Analyze what you believe has happened. We will then take a closer look at this dimension, as well as its implications for business.

What's in a Word?

Critical comments by members of a newly formed, bicultural project team created severe tension and almost led to the breakdown of a project being done across cultures. The team consisted of a group of Italian engineers, who had been sent to the Netherlands to work together with a group of Dutch engineers of an associated company. The team's task was to design a new Personal Intelligent Communicator, a process that would also allow the Italian engineers to learn more about the specific technology of this Personal Intelligent Communicator and its potential problems.

Each day, the Italian engineers met with the Dutch chief engineers to review their part of the project. Initially, those meetings

86 SPECIFIC/DIFFUSE PERSPECTIVES

were very effective. However, after a while, whenever they discussed how to modify and improve the design, frictions arose, which soon developed into severe conflict. The Italian engineers did not mind modifications and improvements as such, as these are common during development work. But they got irritated each time the Dutch chief engineers called their proposals "crazy ideas" or "crazy solutions." Although they knew the Dutch had more expertise in this field, their own ideas and proposals were certainly anything but crazy, as a closer look and analysis would surely reveal.

It did not take long before the conflict escalated. When the Dutch again called the Italians' proposal "crazy," the Italians refused to change anything. The Dutch were responsible for the project and insisted on giving up on that "crazy idea." The Italian engineers left the meeting in anger and frustration. From then on, the team no longer cooperated, and their performance rapidly declined.

The Dutch chief engineer wondered about what had gone wrong and at some point asked his Italian colleagues what had happened. They replied that they just would not accept any longer that their proposals be called "crazy." He replied that he hadn't meant it personally. Apparently, "crazy solution" meant something different to the Italians than to the Dutch.

Discussion Points

- What is the basis of the misunderstanding?
- What advice would you give to the Dutch chief engineer?

Recognizing the Difference Between Specific and Diffuse Orientations

How do we engage in relationships? Do we engage with others in specific areas of life and with specific roles each of us assumes? Or do we get involved in multiple areas, with diffuse roles and expectations about the relationship?

In Specifically Oriented Cultures:

- Managers segregate their task relationship with subordinates from other ways of relating to them.
- Example: Say a manager supervises the sale of integrated circuits. If he were to meet one of his sales reps in the bar, on the golf course, on vacation or in the local store, little of his authority would play a role in how he interacts with the salesperson in those situations. Indeed, he may defer to the sales rep as a more skilled shopper or ask advice on improving his golf game.
- Each type of encounter is considered as independent of the other, that is, as a specific case.

In Diffuse-Oriented Cultures:

- Every life space permeates all other life spaces.
- Example: Madame la directrice is a formidable authority wherever you encounter her. If she runs the company, her subordinates would assume that her opinions on haute cuisine are more informed than theirs. Her taste in clothes and her value as a citizen are all affected by her being the director, and she probably expects to be treated with special respect by those who know her—in the street, the club or a shop.

Although a person's reputation will always influence other areas of life, cultures differ in the extent to which this is the case. The difference in extent is what we measure as a specific orientation (where it is small) vs. a diffuse orientation (where it is large).

Personality as Concentric Circles, Based on the Work of Kurt Lewin

U-Type Circles (U = USA)

- There is a small private space in the center.
- The public space is large.

- The public space is segregated into specific sections: at work, in the bowling club, at the Parent-Teachers' Association, local chapter of the Veterans of Foreign Wars, and so on.
- People who enter a space need not be close to you.
- They may not feel free to call on you unless it is about the specific area where you met.
- Admitting the other to a public layer is not much of a commitment.
- Others can be easily approached in a friendly and open way.
- You "know" the other for limited purposes only.
- Your obligations are confined to these purposes and don't create expectations about others.

G-Type Circle (G = German)
- The public space is large.
- There is a large private space in the center.
- The center space is guarded by a thick line.
- The center space is hard to enter; permission is needed
- Once admitted to the private space, there are diffuse expectations about boundaries.
- Standing and reputation shine across spaces: Professional qualifications say something about you as a person.

Sources for Misperceptions
- Specific people may find diffuse people to be distant and hard to get to know.
- Diffuse people may find specific people to be unjustifiably cheerful, garrulous and superficial.

How Did We Test the Differences Across National Cultures?

Our research shows pronounced differences on this dimension, as illustrated by responses to the following situation (Question 38 of the THT cross-cultural questionnaire).

SPECIFIC/DIFFUSE PERSPECTIVES

A boss asks a subordinate to help him paint his house. The subordinate, who does not feel like doing it, discusses the situation with a colleague.

a) *The colleague argues: "You don't have to paint if you don't feel like it. He is your boss at work. Outside he has little authority."*

b) *The subordinate argues: "Despite the fact that I don't feel like it, I will paint it. He is my boss, and you can't ignore that outside work either."*

In specific societies, with their sharp separation of work and private life, employees are not at all inclined to assist. As one Dutch respondent put it, "House painting is not in my collective labor agreement."

Figure 7.2 shows the proportion of managers who would not paint the house.

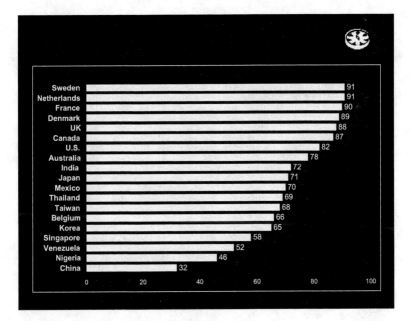

Figure 7.2 Percentage Who Would Not Paint the House

Key Findings

- In the Netherlands and Sweden and in most of Northern Europe, more than 80% of employees would not paint the house.
- In China and Nigeria, the majority would paint the boss's house.
- More than 70% of Japanese employees would not help paint the house: Surprised by the Japanese score, we reinterviewed some Japanese respondents. They replied that in Japan, people hardly ever paint houses! Additional questions used in our research suggest that they tend toward the diffuse end of the dimension.

8
RECONCILING HIGH-CONTEXT WITH LOW-CONTEXT PERSPECTIVES

Context is about how much you need to know before you can communicate effectively and how much shared knowledge is taken for granted. In specific cultures, there is a tendency toward low-context communication, meaning that people are straightforward in their communication regardless of the context they are saying it in. In diffuse cultures, there is a tendency toward high-context communication. Here, people tend to say different things in different contexts, for example, when the boss is there. Or they use one word where the meaning differs depending on the context, such as when an Englishman says something is "interesting."

Strategies for Getting to Know New Business Partners/Strangers in Different Cultures

High-context people tend to "circle around" new business partners. It is important to get to know them diffusely. However, it takes time to establish trust. One is therefore advised to get to the specifics of the business only later. Strangers must be "filled in" before business can be properly discussed. Communications are rich and subtle in their meanings and may carry a lot of "baggage." Foreigners may never really feel comfortable or fully integrated. You do not get trapped in an eight-year relationship with a dishonest partner because you detect any unsavory aspects early on.

In low-context cultures, one can get "straight to the point" by quickly addressing the neutral, "objective" aspects of the business deal. If the other maintains interest, then it is time to learn more about her (i.e., circle outside) in order to facilitate the deal. One believes that relative strangers can quickly share in rule making. Dramatic steps to get strangers involved and up-to-date should be minimized. One tends to be adaptable and flexible. You don't waste time wining and dining a person who is not fully committed to the deal in the first place.

In answering a question, a diffuse-oriented person will give you the background details first before the specific response—first creating the context you need for understanding the significance of the details. Seeing this as "beating around the bush," people with a specific orientation may interrupt to encourage the other to get to the point. As a result, the diffuse-oriented person feels personally attacked. (See Figure 8.1.)

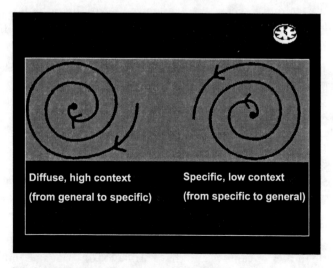

Figure 8.1 Circling Round or Getting Straight to the Point

Written Reports in Diffuse Cultures/High Context:

- Contain sophisticated introductions.
- Include lots of historical background.
- May use difficult language—the reader has to do the work.
- Leave important issues to the end.
- Demonstrate the authority of the author.

Written Reports in Specific Cultures/Low Context:

- Are succinct and brief.
- Have direct, salient conclusions.
- Include an executive summary.
- Use bullet points.
- Use easy language.

Implications for Performance Management

Specific cultures focus on shareholder return for the simple reason that goals and objectives need to be clear and based on financial/quantitative results. With the development of a specific culture, the outside world comes into focus, and results for external shareholders come to the foreground. But then, because of the short-term focus shown in the next quarterly statements, management development programs are pushed to the background.

THT Consulting has run management development programs for many Anglo-Saxon (specific) organizational cultures for more than a decade, only to have them cancel our interventions after just *one* bad financial quarter. What a contrast with some German (diffuse) organizations, where the educational programs were continued despite several bad quarters in succession. In the Finnish organization Partek, we found that financial surplus was reserved for the next year's learning budget, and the learning fed into the operations to improve future financial results. (See Figure 8.2.)

In a European insurance company that we assisted, management became concerned because some very talented high-potential staff

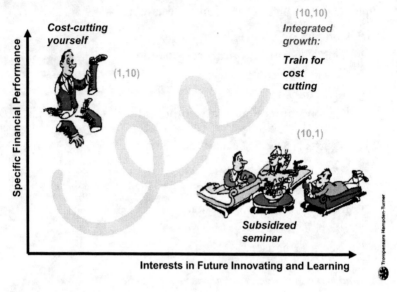

Figure 8.2 From the Balanced to the Integrated Scorecard

started to resign. From the exit interviews, it became clear that the severe budget cuts that followed 9/11—when training programs were the first casualty—were the major factor in people leaving. High-potential people felt neglected—that their expectations of being supported to develop further were not met. The dilemma underlying this incident was obviously not reconciled, and the results were to be expected. But just ignoring concerns about their career development to save costs was not a good idea either.

The CEO reconciled the needs for short-term results and for the development of staff by increasing the training budget by 20% for the year to come. But he had one condition: He required 20% of all training activities to be focused on increasing the bottom line.

When an organization defines "performance," it is necessary to do so in a comprehensive manner. If an assembly line worker is performing repetitive work following prescribed routines, it seems reasonable to base an appraisal on productivity, quality of work and dependability. But if the role of employees on the line is broadened to include additional responsibilities that include problem solving and developing improved methods, it is necessary to ensure that performance is defined and measured in a broader way that includes these responsibilities. If they are not addressed in the appraisal, how can the employee believe management feels they are important? Although the "balanced scorecard" concept has had broad application for executive and managerial employees over the last decade, it seems reasonable to broaden the use of the concept to all employees. Deming advised companies to only hold employees accountable for things they could influence but assumed that accountability would be expected for everything the employee was expected to impact.

A major challenge in performance management when there is considerable cultural diversity in the workforce is deciding how to communicate the appraisal of an employee's performance. In high-context cultures, there is a lot of understanding about what is expected, even though it is not stated openly and explicitly. There is also an unstated agreement about how things like performance assessments should be done. For example, in Japan, it is done indirectly and sometimes through intermediaries. This is an attempt to "save face." But this works only in homogeneous societies and/or where considerable socialization results in a common understanding, even though it is below the surface. Americans often believe Japanese colleagues are evasive or noncommittal, but much of this impression is due to different expectations. A Japanese manager will be more inclined to assume there is a common understanding about the facts and therefore there is no need to directly confront an employee, who will feel diminished and will withdraw from the relationship. American mangers are trained to "tell it like it is" and to write it down for inclusion in the personnel file (just in case the employee sues, claiming discrimination).

96 HIGH-CONTEXT/LOW-CONTEXT PERSPECTIVES

Implications for Reward Management

In specific cultures, it is very important to link specific aspects of performance to specifically defined rewards, such as bonuses. On the contrary, in diffuse cultures, there is a tendency to be more high context in the approach. The whole tends to be taken into consideration, and rewards such as promotions and assigned parking places tend to be considered.

Reconciling Specific and Diffuse Cultures Through the Integrated Scorecard

Back to Qwenchy. Ms. Jones was thinking about this wide range of options. Should one focus only on specific aspects or rather include the whole? In order to try to get the whole group to agree, she proposed the following in a flash of creative genius:

> Gentlemen, we have been quite successful in Qwenchy with the introduction of the balanced scorecard looking at financial performance, developing our people, improving business processes and being more client oriented. But what have we seen these last two years in the midst of the financial crisis? We have focused only on financial performance and improving business processes and have postponed the development of our employees. I don't propose to do the opposite but to try to find an integrated scorecard. Instead of asking our people what they have done to increase efficiency and financial performance, I would have you ask them how they have used the development of their people to increase financial performance and vice versa. Then we don't have to oscillate between extremes over time.

All agreed, and the beginning of an applause was heard. This was going in the right direction. It was a small win but a win nonetheless.

Mr. Khasmi seemed to be relatively happy with the way performance measurement was presented. However, he had one footnote to add: The achievement of results can rarely be totally "objective." Indeed, several aspects play an important role: the difficulty of the fixed target (how much effort that is required) and how much impact an unstable business environment will have on the probability that targets can be reached. On this, Mr. Montovani agreed.

Mr. Yakomoto reiterated he was opposed to the idea of paying solely for performance. He argued that in Japan, lifetime employment is still on offer, and the rewards lie much more in the long-term career possibilities than in short-term cash awards. "Yes, that might be the case," replies Jones, "but we need also to support the idea of controlling the cost of rewards by rewarding only the higher performers. Those are by definition the people who work the hardest. You feel you need to praise and reward them for that."

9
RECONCILING ACHIEVEMENT WITH ASCRIPTION PERSPECTIVES

This dimension of culture deals with an orientation that accords status to people based on their achievements or that ascribe status to people based on their title, age, gender, social connections/class, education or profession. People with an *achievement* orientation will expect the performance to be measured and rewarded based on what they accomplish and contribute to the organization. People with an *ascription* orientation will expect to have their personal characteristics considered when performance is measured and rewarded. Countries with an achievement culture include America, Canada, England and the Scandinavian countries. Countries with an ascription culture include many in Asia and the Middle East, as well as some in Latin countries.

Status by Achievement and Economic Development

An achievement orientation, with status based on performing-well criteria, is often seen as part of "modernization" and thus as key to economic and business success. The idea is that, once you start rewarding business achievement, the process is self-perpetuating. People work hard to gain social esteem, resulting in a so-called achieving society, and a performance culture forms. This orientation is strongly based on Protestantism, which embraces the pursuit

100   ACHIEVEMENT/ASCRIPTION PERSPECTIVES

of spiritual justification through hard work, which long ago gave achievers a religious sanction. Capitalism is its driving force.

Societies that award status based on ascription (i.e., based on Being criteria), are often economically backward, because their reasons for assigning status do not facilitate commercial success. This would hold for Catholic and Hindu countries, and also for Buddhist countries with the teachings of detachment from earthly concerns.

How Do We Measure the Status Orientation in Different Cultures?

We collected responses to the following statements, using a 5-point scale (1 = strongly agree, 5 = strongly disagree):

1.   *The most important thing in life is to think and act in the ways that best suit the way you really are, even if you do not get things done.*

The second statement looked at the importance of family background:

2.   *The respect a person gets is highly dependent on their family background.*

Key Findings

Figures 9.1 and 9.2 show the percentage of participants who disagree with these two statements.

- Countries in which only a minority agrees that "getting things done" is the most important (see Figure 9.1) are, broadly speaking, being-oriented cultures.
- In the U.S., Australia and Canada, a majority opted for the doing approach—deciding in favor of getting things done at the expense of acting the way that best suits you.
- The U.S. is clearly a culture in which status is mainly based on doing (see Figure 9.2): 76% of Americans disagree that status should depend on family background.
- Both figures indicate that achievement orientation and type of religion correlate.

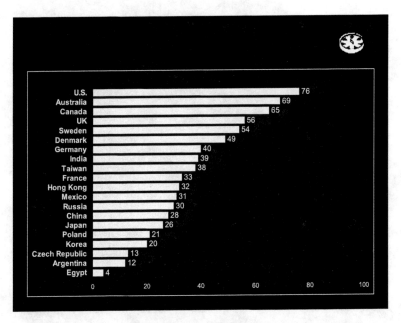

Figure 9.1 Doing vs. Being—Quality of Life Is Acting as It Suits You: Percentage of Respondents Who Disagree That One Should Always Act in the Way That Best Suits the Way One Is

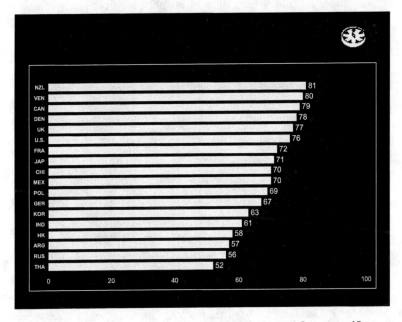

Figure 9.2 Doing vs. Being—Status Comes from Family Background: Percentage of Respondents Who Disagree with the Fact That the Respect a Person Gets Is Highly Dependent on His/Her Family Background

102   ACHIEVEMENT/ASCRIPTION PERSPECTIVES

Implications for Performance Management

If an organization bases its appraisal of an employee's performance solely on what has been achieved in the current period, it provides motivation to perform at the highest possible level and may be viewed as the appropriate measure of contribution, since this approach does not consider other factors that may be viewed as irrelevant. This conveys a your-value-depends-on-what-you-have-accomplished-lately message to employees.

When who an individual is or the status he is ascribed influences evaluation of performance, it confirms that the person is due certain treatment, as a result of their personal characteristics or what capabilities they possess. One source of ascribed status is perceived potential. Employees with an assumed high potential, due to their education, experience and standing in their field, will be recognized as being capable of making contributions, and this perception may cause the organization to assume that poor results are attributable to outside factors beyond the employee's control. This often is the result of programs that afford special treatment to "high potentials" being adopted by organizations.

Potential is a prerequisite for performing, but having the knowledge, skills and abilities to perform at high levels does not constitute performance. Due to a lack of effort or a lack of focus on things that would produce the desired results for the organization, a highly capable person may not perform well. The organization has a responsibility to utilize the capabilities of individuals, and if someone is performing at a level below his potential, the cause may be a lack of opportunity to utilize that potential. The organization must ensure that the individual is placed in a suitable role, that the required resources are made available and that the motivation to perform is provided. The individual has a responsibility to utilize her capabilities in a manner that benefits the organization, which includes expending the required effort and focusing on what will contribute to organizational success.

Implications for Rewards Management

If employees are rewarded based on their current performance, it encourages them to perform well. But if others are rewarded similarly because of their personal characteristics, it may create feelings of inequity and may send the message that rewards are not appropriately distributed on an equitable basis. An employee who achieves more than others and is accorded higher status but rewarded less may begin to question the organization's commitment to rewarding performance.

If merit pay programs base increases on both the performance and the position of the employee's pay rate in their assigned pay range, it will be necessary to justify both the equity of the assigned pay ranges and the performance ratings. If an employee with many years in the job is classified on a higher level in the occupational ladder than a more junior person who is actually more competent, it will raise questions about the equity of the classification. If the individuals are assigned to classification levels based solely on seniority, it conveys the message that longevity rather than performance drives rewards. A more junior person who has acquired the same level of competence in the field is likely to believe that he should be classified in the same level as the more senior person. Because the pay range for the higher classification level will result in higher pay for the more senior person, even if both receive the same percentage of pay, an inequity will still be seen as existing.

To reconcile this dilemma, the organization must ensure that employees who receive higher pay because of their longevity bring value to the organization through their greater knowledge of the work of the organization. A separate longevity pay can be put into place as a supplement to the merit pay, which would send the message that service is also valued by the organization. This would enable the organization to reward performance appropriately through merit pay adjustments, while recognizing the value of loyalty. An example of where organizational knowledge has value would be a water

ACHIEVEMENT/ASCRIPTION PERSPECTIVES

utility. People familiar with the inner workings of the older equipment would know how to deal with issues that are not addressed in the computer records, since they were modified before there were computers. This may enable them to avoid mistakes that would have been made by those lacking the detailed knowledge.

Reconciling Achievement and Ascription

Back to Qwenchy. Mr. Mantovani asked for the group to listen to his Italian experience with a high-potential program that met with great success. The young graduates were selected on their potential to grow to top leadership positions in the organization within 15 years' time. That is pretty fast in a typical Italian context. "We throw these youngsters into a tough environment where they have to show how good they are in fierce competition with others. In other words, we earmark them as HiPos [high potentials] and thus attribute status to them, but that status is maintained only if they show they deserve it." Mr. Yakomoto nods and says, "We in Japan have the same type of program for our students who come from the University of Tokyo. It is a highly prestigious program where we expect the utmost performance."

Ms. Jones concluded by saying, "Often in the U.S., it is the opposite. You first work hard regardless of your background, and if you do well for some years, you will be rewarded appropriately in the long run. Should we not adopt this meritocracy approach at Qwenchy?"

Mr. Khasmi expressed a new concern that fixed performance targets may be unrealistic, given the influence of the unstable UAE business environment. He pointed out that in Islamic cultures, the *inshallah* belief ("if Allah wills it") has a significant impact on people's motivation to strive. If it is God's will, rather than one's effort, that determines performance, then why should an employee strive to meet the goals that drive performance ratings and rewards?

10
RECONCILING INTERNALLY CONTROLLED WITH EXTERNALLY CONTROLLED PERSPECTIVES

This dimension of culture deals with beliefs about whether individuals have control over results or external factors have an impact on results. People with an *internal control* orientation have a can-do attitude and believe that concerted effort and application of their knowledge and skills will enable them to deal with issues and to produce the desired results. Countries with internal control orientations are mostly North American and Western European, and the people there believe that nature can be controlled by human effort. People with an *external control* orientation tend to believe that things outside their control will have a significant impact on what they are able to accomplish, and they believe that human actions must be in harmony with nature. Countries with external control orientations are mostly Asian, Eastern European and Middle Eastern. There is also a tendency to believe that luck has a lot to do with results in some Asian cultures. On the other hand, lucky Americans are inclined to attribute success to their own efforts.

106 INTERNALLY/EXTERNALLY CONTROLLED PERSPECTIVES

Recognizing the Differences Between Internal vs. External Controlled Orientation

This dimension of culture captures the different views that people hold regarding their natural environment. From the beginning, people have struggled against nature's elements: wind, floods, fire, cold, earthquakes, famine, pests and predators. Survival always meant acting on the environment in ways that render it both less threatening and more sustaining, making constant action an inescapable necessity.

Internal Control Orientation

- People believe they can and should control nature by imposing their will upon it.
- They seek to comprehend nature by equating it with mechanisms that can be regulated.
- Organizations are conceived of as machines, manipulated by the decisions of its operators.

External Control Orientation

- People are part of nature and must go along with its laws, directions and forces.
- They see organizations as a product of nature and believe that isomorphism with the environment is necessary to maintain ecological balance.

How Do We Assess Cultural Differences in Control Orientation? The Rotter Scale

The American psychologist J. B. Rotter developed a scale to measure "locus of control": He found that people with an internal locus of control were typically more successful Americans, while those with an external locus of control were often less successful Americans, disadvantaged by their circumstances or shaped by the competitive efforts of their rivals.

INTERNALLY/EXTERNALLY CONTROLLED PERSPECTIVES 107

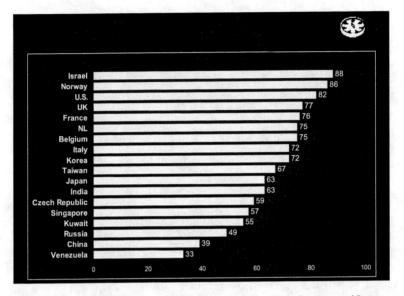

Figure 10.1 Internal vs. External Control—Making Your Plans Work: Percentage of Respondents Who Think That They Can Make Their Plans Work

We used several items of the Rotter scale to test for cultural differences in how people relate to natural events. The questions all take the form of alternatives; managers were asked to select the statement they believed best reflected reality.

Figure 10.1 shows the percentage of respondents who chose Statement A (Internal Control Orientation) when asked to choose between the following (Question 46 from the cross-cultural questionnaire):

Of the following two statements, which do you believe to be more in line with reality?

  a) *When I make plans, I am almost certain that I can make them work (Internal Control).*
  b) *It is not always wise to plan too far ahead because many things turn out to be a matter of good or bad fortune anyhow (External Control).*

Key Findings

- Most Western countries score high on internal control.
- In the U.S., 82% of managers believe they control their own destinies.
- Of the Dutch, 75% believe they control their own destiny.
- In Asia, the score is more diverse:
  - 39% of Chinese respondents agree with Statement A.
  - 63% of Japanese respondents agree with Statement A.

Implications of the Two Perspectives for Business

People with a Sense of Internal Control:

- Tend to favor a mechanistic view of nature.
- Believe that nature can be controlled once its elements and the rules of their interaction are understood.
- See the goal as being to develop suitable instruments for manipulating nature.
- See themselves as influencing their environment, not vice versa.
- See personal power as a common instrument of control.
- Believe obstacles are there to be overcome.
- Think that influencing others is a normal aspect of the general influence that man has on nature.
- Believe concentrating on things that one is good at ("playing to one's strengths"), can help them persuade others to accept what they want.
- Favor strategies like "technology push."
- Accept that conflicts are common in the perpetual struggle to influence the environment.
- Accept that conflicts are part of doing business, especially if business is conceived as a win/lose game.

People with a Sense of External Control:

- Favor an organic view of nature.
- See people as being subjugated to nature's dynamics and forces.

INTERNALLY/EXTERNALLY CONTROLLED PERSPECTIVES 109

- See that being in harmony with the environment means being in balance with nature.
- Seek harmony when defining which actions are right and which are wrong.
- Feel that conflict signals that we don't understand nature's forces and thus act against them—a fight we cannot win.
- Consider uncontrollable, unpredictable things like luck, change and fate to determine the cause of events.
- Focus on responding to the environment and to the needs of the customers.
- Favor strategies of "market pull."
- Perceive a person attempting to control nature as aggressive and dominant.
- See conflicts caused by such actions as direct proof of having made the wrong decision.

Implications for Performance Management

In order to have the motivation to attempt to meet or exceed performance standards, employees must have the confidence that they can accomplish what is asked of them. Those employees who believe in internal control think they have the required knowledge, skills and abilities to produce the desired results. But they must also believe that the organization will provide the necessary resources (time, staff, budget, autonomy), will acknowledge the results and will reward them appropriately in order to be motivated to perform at high levels. Their belief is that they are in control.

If employees think that external factors will have a dominant impact on outcomes, it is unlikely that they will expend their best efforts. They will believe that no matter what they do, the outcome is not achievable, except by luck or by divine will.

It is incumbent on the organization to reconcile its desire for specific outcomes with employee beliefs about whether they are able to produce the desired results. If performance standards are set at an unachievable level, motivation to extend effort will not exist.

110 INTERNALLY/EXTERNALLY CONTROLLED PERSPECTIVES

If managers attribute success to outside factors or their competent supervision rather than to the employee's efforts, the employee will believe the target will be moved after they have released their arrow. And if employees are uncertain about what the expectations are, they will just do their best to do what they think is required, which is unlikely to be focused on the right things.

There is considerable behavioral research on Western (internal control culture) subjects indicating that managers are more inclined to believe that if employees succeed, it is more due to environmental conditions, while employees tend to believe it is due to their efforts. Although similar research on external control cultures has not been done, there is anecdotal evidence that both managers and employees will attribute success or failure to external conditions rather than to an employee's motivation to perform. When an organization attempts to impose a performance management system globally based on an internal control philosophy, it must be cautious to determine whether its effectiveness will be diminished in cultures with an external control orientation.

Implications for Rewards Management

If an organization commits to basing rewards on specific levels of performance, it must define performance using criteria and standards that employees believe are achievable. The employees must also believe rewards are in an appropriate proportion to the value of the outcomes produced. By doing so, it enables the organization to reward employees when it is justified and not to reward them if the standards are not met. Merit pay and incentive plans must be based on achieving predetermined results in order to be credible. It is also important to ensure that the individual believes that he or she can produce or at least contribute to aggregated results if incentive plans operate at the team/unit/organizational levels. Employees with little autonomy and acting under direct supervision may find it difficult to believe they can impact organization-wide or even group/unit results. In order to provide motivation to perform, the organization must establish a believable link between what the individual does and the aggregated results or at least convince the employees that, if everyone performs well in their assigned roles, it will positively impact aggregated performance.

Some organizations operate in environments that constrain their performance, such as those in highly regulated industries. Other organizations function under highly uncertain conditions that have a major impact on their performance. Even in cultures that have an inner-directed orientation, it is important not to make employee rewards overly dependent on results when no matter what they do or how hard they try, the environmental conditions will determine results. Deming stressed the need to hold employees accountable for things they controlled and not to judge them based on things controlled by the systems they worked with.

A reconciliation of the dilemma produced by employees having an outer-directed orientation is for the organization to convince employees to put forth their best efforts and to focus them on the goals of the organization. If employees believe that divine will determines outcomes, they should be convinced that their personal capabilities are a gift and that it is their responsibility to use them to the best of their ability.

Dilemma: Focus on External Customers vs. Focus on Internal Processes

To create sustainable business success, we also need to improve the internal processes through the involvement of customers. Co-development programs, where suppliers align strategically with their clients, are a great example. Applied Materials, as one of the main suppliers of microchips, has used this approach very effectively. Their survival is completely dependent on codeveloping microchips with AMD and Intel. This is quite different from "balance" (as in the balanced scorecard). It supposes that value is not added by having

112 INTERNALLY/EXTERNALLY CONTROLLED PERSPECTIVES

high scores in each of the four perspectives and then adding them up. Rather, it needs the added extra from a win/win solution that derives from the cross-integration of past and future, internal and external values.

Internal Processes vs. External Customers

A case in point is the Dutch electronics giant Philips. It faced the second, reoccurring strategic dilemma of innovation: the well recognized tension between technology push and market pull. Do we make something we want and know how to make and then try to find a market to sell it? Or do we let the demands and wants of customers feed back into our R&D and product planning?

For many years, a pure push from technology worked successfully in internally controlled societies such as the UK, the Netherlands and the U.S. in the 20 years following World War II due to demand exceeding supply. However, technology push was doomed to failure when internationalization accelerated in the 1960s. American-produced and -conceived consumer electronics were wiped out by foreign competition, and Japanese products took their place. A push strategy can work, however, especially in situations of low competition. In cases where competition is strong, this push approach leads to selling your fantastic products in niche markets to early adapter/purchasers with a high disposable income. As it happens, this market has too few customers to be a viable source of the required volume or adequate and sustainable profitability.

Dutch Philips is a splendid example of an organization that still struggles with the marketing of high-end products such as the CD and DVD. Philips invents and Sony sells, say the cynics. It is typically Japanese to be fully empathetic with the customer. But this extreme "market pull" approach also has its restrictions because customers often have no idea what they want.

Bang & Olufsen also faced challenges when attempting to develop an understanding of the evolving market and patterns of

INTERNALLY/EXTERNALLY CONTROLLED PERSPECTIVES 113

demand, before aligning its own products with this knowledge. "We had to teach people how to think in business terms, without sacrificing their pride in their creativity and their products," CEO Anders Knutsen recalled. "Beauty, style and technical superiority had been everything in the past. No one had been paying attention to development costs or commercial success." Knutsen regarded this imbalance as so serious that he made himself the Head of Marketing and Sales until an internationally experienced VP could be found. In this way, he was able to rediscover facts that the company had ignored for too long.

"Bang & Olufsen thought communication was a one-way process, and that its customers were dealers, not consumers. Of course, the dealers were passing on our arrogant treatment to the final customers," observed Knutsen. He had discovered that dealers used the Bang & Olufsen aura to upgrade the image of their dealerships, while putting most of their energies into selling rival products better suited to the market, including Philips, Daewoo, Sony and Grundig. These appeared reasonably priced when compared to Bang & Olufsen's expensive, up-market offerings. "There was a radical disconnection between the product and the market," he recalls. "It was as if we communicated with the product and not with the people."

Using THT Consulting WebCue tools, senior executives from Bang & Olufsen framed this dilemma in their own words as:

The Disconnection of Sales and Marketing from Research, Development and Production and the elevation of the latter functions to a dominant position, so that Scorecard marketing commercial considerations were largely ignored.[1]

The integrated scorecard approach is intended to overcome the linear restrictions of the balanced scorecard. The intention is not so much to criticize it as to improve it and to offer the reader a vehicle

114 INTERNALLY/EXTERNALLY CONTROLLED PERSPECTIVES

for making dilemma reconciliation tangible and practical. Corporate cultures often refuse, point blank, to value both ends of these polarities equally. You cannot order them to do so. You can only show them that learning goals subsequently improve financials by a specific (x) amount. Some of the perils of "imbalance" and the benefits of "balance" are depicted in Figure 10.2.

A company can be paralyzed by analysis or by "lean and mean" cost-cutting (top left in both figures). It can also indulge itself in subsidized seminars and become the customer's creature, ignoring its own internal standards (bottom right of both figures). Or it can grow innovatively. Such growth requires more than balance. It requires a fusion and reconciliation of such contrasting values.

Back to Qwenchy. "It seems to me that we ought to be concerned about another characteristic of the local environment," said Mr. Khasmi. "We've talked about whether employees believe they are in control of the outcomes or whether external factors impact what they can achieve. But there is also the issue of how the organization is structured. Is it a formal hierarchy with prescribed amounts of latitude assigned to each level, or are employees expected to take the initiative to assume autonomy?"

"Yes," responded Mr. Yakamoto, "we are careful to ensure that employees do not outgrow their britches, to use an American term, which can result in superiors being left out of the decision even though they will be held accountable for the results. That would be unacceptable in our culture."

"The control freaks are at it again," thought Ms. Jones to herself. She had experienced what seemed like endless delays in getting relatively minor policy changes approved in both the Middle Eastern and Asian regions. They say they have to go through an extensive process when decisions are made in order to ensure that all those who must implement the decisions have had input into them and accept the result. Several of the Asian HR people had mocked the American approach, which in their mind was to make quick decisions and

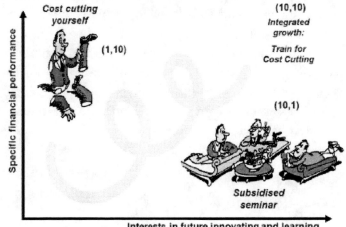

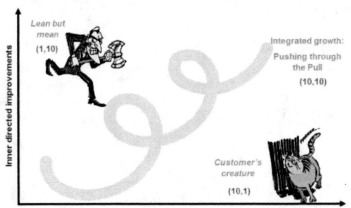

Figure 10.2 Two Examples of the Dangers and Benefits of Balancing the Score Card

116 INTERNALLY/EXTERNALLY CONTROLLED PERSPECTIVES

then experience endless delays in implementation, due to the lack of buy-in by all parties. She did accept that a performance management system should include giving employees an appropriate amount of autonomy in setting goals and deciding how to achieve them. But this might be unrealistic if their unit was vertically structured with specific processes for decision making. Qwenchy had been emphasizing a more egalitarian approach to structure and decision making in its corporate development center courses, but it was clear that the degree to which this philosophy was being accepted varied widely across regions and cultures.

Note

1. Fons Trompenaars and Peter Woolliams, *Marketing Across Cultures*, Wiley, 2005, pp. 286–287.

11
RECONCILING HIERARCHICAL WITH EGALITARIAN PERSPECTIVES

This dimension of culture deals with an orientation to deference to authority in a hierarchical structure or to more equality in an egalitarian structure. Those from cultures that expect large distances between managers and subordinates will respect titles and status and will accept direction from those higher in the structure. Country cultures that tend to be hierarchical include China, Mexico and Japan, as well as others in Asia and Latin America. Those from cultures that feel everyone has a role to play will tend to feel free to participate in decisions and to lead activities when they have the most relevant expertise. Country cultures that tend to be egalitarian include the U.S., UK and most of the countries in Western Europe and the Scandinavian region.

Implications for Performance Management

The degree to which deference to authority is expected will have an impact on whether employees are expected to participate in setting their goals and in determining how to achieve those goals. In cultures where power is expected to be concentrated at higher levels, employees may have very limited autonomy and may feel their role is to carry out the directions given to them. Performance appraisal will tend to be a very top-down process, with the manager establishing performance criteria and standards and evaluating how well a subordinate did relative to those standards. And in this type of culture, the subordinate would not be expected to contest the judgment of the manager.

In cultures where employees are expected to play an active role in establishing goals and in deciding how to meet them, the performance appraisal process will tend to be an interactive joint effort and the employee will be expected to voice opinions that might differ from the manager's assessment. The employee is expected to report results and to identify issues continuously to the manager, who will work with the employee to determine how issues can be resolved and the desired results achieved.

One approach to reconciling the dilemmas presented by the contrast between a hierarchical approach and an egalitarian approach is to recognize that authority must be clearly vested so that decisions can be made efficiently and effectively. But this must be done while ensuring that employees at all levels have an appropriate amount of input and that decision making occurs at the level where the required knowledge exists. Performance management systems should include the setting of objectives but also engage employees in deciding how they are to be met, to the extent appropriate. In dynamic environments, decisions may have to be made quickly, and routing information through tall hierarchies may delay the decisions and result in lost opportunities or suboptimal results.

Implications for Rewards Management

Rewarding employees based on outcomes over which they did not have full control raises issues relative to motivation and satisfaction. If the employees are resigned to the concentration of authority at higher levels in the organization, they may feel there is no reason to extend their best efforts, inasmuch as their recommendations are unlikely to be given consideration. And when the workforce is culturally diverse, this will generally result in acceptance by some and dissatisfaction on the part of others. Of course, the same disconnect may occur when an egalitarian approach to management is employed: Those from hierarchical cultures will expect to be given specific direction and to follow directions, and when this type of guidance is lacking, they may lose faith in their managers. When there is a gap between expectations and reality, issues are created that, if not recognized and properly dealt with, can lessen motivation and create dissatisfaction.

The rewards strategy selected by an organization should fit its philosophy regarding who can and should impact performance at all levels. Bureaucratic cultures usually lead to vertical hierarchies, where authority follows the status assigned to the roles of individuals. For example, if incentive compensation is used, a hierarchical structure will usually result in eligibility for rewards being determined by organizational level. Conversely, in an egalitarian structure, it is possible that authority will follow expertise when decisions are made. A software designer responsible for adopting an innovative approach in a new product may be rewarded handsomely for the contribution, even though the person is at a relatively low position in the organization chart. Had that designer been imbedded in a hierarchical structure, the credit for the innovation would likely accrue to the person with the formal responsibility for the unit, although some of the reward may "trickle down" to the person actually making the contribution. In fact, if the designer had been imbedded in a rigid hierarchy, the innovation may not have been adopted at all due to resistance on the part of those managing the person. Although the trend in Western cultures over the last several decades has been to disburse authority on these types of decisions to those best able to make them, this has not spread to other cultures.

Back to Qwenchy. Mr. Yamamoto suggested that two other perspectives should be considered before the adoption of a single approach to defining, measuring and rewarding performance. "We tend to differ across countries and regions when it comes to focusing on the past, the present or the future. We also have differing perspectives about defining performance in the short term or the long term. These seem to be very important differences when considering the adoption of a single approach."

"Yes, I agree fully," chimed in Mr. Khasmi.

"And I concur," added Mr. Montovani.

"Oh, boy!" thought Ms. Jones. "Daniels has been put in the hole this bunch dug, and now they're filling in the hole with dirt. Wonder if they will at least put flowers on the top."

12
RECONCILING PAST, PRESENT AND FUTURE PERSPECTIVES

This dimension of culture deals with an orientation to the past, the present or the future. People with an orientation to the past will view the present and the future as an extension of the past. They tend to set current and future performance standards by extending a trend line from past performance, and current and future actions will be aimed at preserving a past identity. Countries with a past orientation include most countries in Southern Europe and Latin America.

People with a present orientation will focus on results measured against current standards and on using time efficiently, with performance measured against established timelines. Objectives will usually be established for the near future, and performance in the next period will be measured against those objectives in that period. Cultures with a present orientation include most North American and Northern European countries.

Cultures with a future orientation will use planning cycles that are long or unbounded and will focus on aspirations and opportunities. Current capabilities will be assessed against what will be needed in the future, and plans will be created to reshape them so they meet the challenges associated with the future. Cultures with a future orientation are most often found in the Asian region,

122 PAST, PRESENT AND FUTURE PERSPECTIVES

although local cultures subscribing to a future orientation are found even in North America. Chief Joseph, leader of a Native American tribe in the U.S., once stated that decisions should be made based on their impact on the seventh generation out, and some tribal councils still subscribe to that approach.

Implications for Performance Management

When establishing performance standards, the frame of reference can be what has been done in the past, what is currently needed or what will be needed in the future. An orientation to the past will tend to result in metrics that are an extension of past results. An organization that sets sales targets as a percentage of past sales defines performance as "doing better." An orientation to the present will tend to result in metrics that are based on current needs. An organization that sets return-on-investment targets based on the current expectations of shareholders and management will disconnect those targets from what happened before and what needs to happen in the future, defining performance as "doing what is necessary today." An orientation to the future will tend to result in metrics developed through a planning process, often using scenario-based planning methods. The standards will be based on future aspirations and projections.

When an employee's performance is appraised, a manager may be influenced by the history of the employee. It may be difficult to appraise performance as being unacceptable if the employee has always done well, even if current performance is truly unacceptable. Managers inherit people who have been given appraisals given by different people, and there is a danger that the current manager has higher standards or that past managers have distorted reality to avoid conflict—or to get rid of the employee by dealing the person to another department. A manager who allows past ratings to influence the current rating can be repeating those past distortions.

PAST, PRESENT AND FUTURE PERSPECTIVES   123

When a manager appraises performance based solely on current results measured against current standards, the appraisal will accurately reflect current realities. However, an employee who has had a bad year after many years of good performance may believe that considering past performance is the fair thing to do. In some cases, the job requirements will have changed and the employee may be less suited to performing well under the new circumstances. Considering past performance may result in a distorted rating based on current performance. Managers may also rightfully consider the competence and the effort level of the employee when rating current performance and might adjust the rating to reflect unanticipated events that were out of the employee's control and that had a significant impact on current results.

Managers may also consider the potential (or their belief about the potential) of an employee when rating current performance. But this may result in a distorted rating of current performance and may turn out to be a poor subjective judgment. Other employees who have performed better in the current period may view their rating relative to the elevated rating of the person viewed as having great potential, thereby causing dissatisfaction.

Implications for Rewards Management

"What you measure and reward you most surely will get more of." If an organization is focused on maintaining consistency and improving on past performance, it could create funds for rewards that are based on a compounded improvement formula. If it is focused on performing in the current period, it could base the size of the rewards fund on current performance measured against current standards. And if it is focused on meeting longer-term objectives or changing its strategy, the fund should be based on either achieving interim targets that will eventually lead to meeting future goals, funding rewards when the future goals are met, or a combination of both.

124 PAST, PRESENT AND FUTURE PERSPECTIVES

Organizations with relatively consistent missions and standards would be most likely to create a trend line that measures relative performance, extending the line from past performance, through the present and into the future. For example, a profit-sharing plan could create a fund that was a percentage of payroll, based on improvement over the past year. An organization that is publicly traded might set standards each year and communicate those to the investment community. An organization that needs to transform itself by changing its mix of products or markets may set longer-term goals and provide the prospect of future rewards contingent on meeting the objectives.

Merit pay programs should ideally be tied to current results vs. current standards. If managers consider past performance or what they think employees are capable of, they vary from what constitutes fair rewards for current performance. The same principle holds true for individual incentive plans that are based on current performance. However, if current performance is to be compared to what has been produced in the past or to what is needed in the future, incentive plans may result in rewards tied to that definition of performance.

13
RECONCILING SHORT-TERM WITH LONG-TERM PERSPECTIVES

This dimension of culture is related to the past-present-future dimension. It deals with an orientation to focusing on either short-term results or long-term results. The short-term view supports viewing current performance as the key to success, while the long-term view supports achieving optimal performance over an extended time frame. Countries with cultures that have a short-term focus include those in North America, while those with a longer-term focus include most countries in Asia.

Implications for Performance Management

One of the key decisions that must be made when defining performance is to establish the measurement time frame. A worker operating a machine producing parts can be evaluated on weekly, daily or even hourly output, while the performance of a manager in charge of building a plant might not be apparent for several years. In some industries, it is difficult to meaningfully determine performance in time frames shorter than an annual accounting cycle, even though monthly and quarterly performance figures are mandated. For some types of work, such as pure research, performance may not be measurable in a meaningful way for several years.

In cultures emphasizing short-term results, organizations may focus on immediate results but do so in a manner that is not sustainable over the long term. In cultures emphasizing performance over the long term, current opportunities may be overlooked or undervalued and may be lost. Reconciling the measurement time frame dilemma can be accomplished by replacing an either/or mind-set with a both/and mind-set. By recognizing that both time frames may be important for some types of work, management may develop appraisals that evaluate not only short-term results but also the impact on the way the results were produced on the longer-term performance of the organization.

Implications for Rewards Management

Cultures that emphasize short-term results tend to reward employees for performing during the current performance period (hour, day, week, month, year). Merit pay systems typically reward performance on an annual basis. Individual incentives based on tangible output often reward performance on a monthly or weekly basis. Commissions and sales incentives are often paid out on a quarterly or monthly basis. Group and organization-wide incentives are usually based on annual performance.

There are also long-term incentive plans, paid in either cash or stock. The long-term plans are most often limited to executives and those managing multiyear projects. The stock-based plans use either options or grants, and their value is tied to the stock price performance rather than to individual or group/organizational performance. Reconciling the measurement time frame dilemma can be done in the same manner used for performance management. Replacing an either/or mind-set with a both/and mind-set will enable an organization to recognize that both time frames may be important for some types of work and for some employees. By aligning the timing of rewards with the measurement of performance, on whatever time frame, the organization can encourage a focus on both short- and long-term performance.

14
ACHIEVING CONSENSUS THROUGH RECONCILIATION

The Qwenchy Country HR Manager task force had submitted its recommendations after the series of meetings, and the new system was based on their input. It had been decided to allow considerable local differentiation initially, while committing to finding common features that would work reasonably well everywhere and standardizing those features.

Mr. Daniels reconvened the task force that had worked on the staff appraisal and reward system some six months later in order to obtain their input on a new HR initiative taking place at Qwenchy. The organization had retained an outside consultant to evaluate how well the performance and rewards management strategy fit different types of employees. The consultant had used a model to pose the question, "Use the same strategy for everyone or different strategies for different businesses and different types of employees?" The model suggested two alternative philosophies: (1) attempt to use one strategy and modify it only if there were compelling reasons to do so, or (2) formulate the ideal "best fit" strategies for each identifiable employee group and then decide to what extent the strategies would be combined. The consultant used the book *Rewarding Performance: Guiding Principles; Custom Strategies* as the basis for this process.[1] (See Figure 14.1.)

Figure 14.1 Global Organization

Mr. Daniels posed an initial question to the group: "You have all pointed out how your cultures make strategies effective or ineffective. Is this true for all types of employees, or does aligning with culture demand less customization for different types?"

Several of the members of the task force seemed puzzled by the question. After all, people are people, so what difference did it make if they were executives or support staff? They all agreed that the types of rewards programs differed—more long-term incentives for executives, more short-term incentives for sales personnel—but wouldn't the performance management be the same? "That is what we are trying to determine," offered Daniels. "Our first session on philosophy created an interesting model. We asked ourselves how performance should be defined for each level of employee and found that the relative emphasis on individual, group/unit and

CONSENSUS THROUGH RECONCILIATION 129

	Organization	Unit	Individual
Top executives	100%	0%	0%
Mid-management	50%	50%	0%
Professional/ supervisory	25%	50%	25%
Other individuals	25%	25%	50%

Figure 14.2 Relative Pay Awards Based on Performance

organization-wide performance should differ across levels. We created a model that we felt was appropriate for each level when weighting the different performance results." (See Figure 14.2.)

"I am surprised you could get Americans to accept that everything should not be determined on their individual performance," interjected Mr. Yakamoto.

"We also agreed that using subjective judgments to measure some dimensions of performance was appropriate," responded Daniels proudly.

Mr. Mantovani thought they must have taken a trip to Italy and added, "Would they accept that feelings could also come to the surface?"

Mr. Daniels, who was onto the cultural baiting by now, responded, "Yes, and we encouraged them to shout and slam the desk while waving their arms at least two or three times during the appraisal meeting!" Because the members of the group had come to respect each other, this produced laughter.

"We are especially concerned about the executives and middle management personnel when we questioned ourselves about the impact of differing cultures, since they are the ones we typically send on extended expatriate assignments," Daniels continued. "If a member of our global cadre is likely to move from one country

CONSENSUS THROUGH RECONCILIATION

to another, we have already adopted policies that adjust for what performance measures are most appropriate to use, how their compensation will be taxed, their relative living costs and the like. Our headquarters-based balanced scorecard approach addresses that. But how do cultural differences impact whether local national peers will accept that their compensation is fair and competitive relative to the expatriates and third country nationals?"

"I believe you have handled this well by using expatriates only when the skills are absent locally and that their tours have been kept short," responded Mr. Yakomoto. "And you do make it clear that they are expected to begin training their local replacement as soon as they arrive," he added. The rest of the group agreed that this limited the resentment of expatriate rewards packages. But they also said that one of the challenges they continued to face was evaluating the performance of expatriates who were not at the general manager level. The policy was that the performance evaluation was to be done by the person's manager in the host country, with consultation provided by the home country manager and corporate HR.

Daniels had tracked these situations and found there to be potential problems if an expatriate comes from a different culture than what prevails in the host country. The communitarian local manager may weight cooperativeness heavily when doing the appraisal while the individualistic expatriate will contend that tangible results should be weighted heavily. In matrixed structures where the expatriate has both a host country evaluator and a home country evaluator, this has often caused the two evaluators to rate differently, based on the factors they consider and the weight they give them.

"And your salespeople who come from the U.S. act as if they are the only ones in the company—free agents, to be measured only based on their sales volume," added Mr. Yamamoto. "They do not seem to understand that how they make sales has great impact on the people who must fulfill orders and handle customer relations. And they don't acknowledge the contribution support people make

CONSENSUS THROUGH RECONCILIATION 131

to their success." Daniels knew that was coming. They had that same problem with American sales reps in the U.S.

"So what should our strategy be for salespeople?" asked Daniels. He knew that they had pressured sales management to consider factors other than sales volume at headquarters, but there was still a question about how well that was working. They had implemented systems that tracked customer satisfaction, repeat business and the share of customer expenditures that Qwenchy was able to capture. But many sales managers had relegated these factors to a minor consideration when evaluating performance. The company had instituted a supplemental incentive plan for sales personnel based on subjective factors, intending to increase the prominence of subjective measures. But when determining what portion of the bonus was impacted by these measures, managers varied widely in how they interpreted plan provisions. And now he had to consider what impact cultural differences would have.

"Why shouldn't the general manager of the country unit be allowed to decide how sales representatives and sales management are measured and rewarded?" asked Mr. Klaus. "We trust our GM to run the business in Germany, so why not trust him to figure out the best way to motivate the sales personnel?" There was substantial agreement in the group, and it seemed that was the best approach because rarely were sales personnel transferred across country units. Daniels felt that if some of the GMs stressed gross sales volumes, others net sales volumes and others balanced sales and qualitative measures, this would be OK.

Daniels then asked the group about how well the performance and rewards systems worked for professional employees. In the U.S., the chief challenge was getting IT and engineering people to create "good enough" product designs rather than shooting for "as good as they can possibly be." The latter approach drove costs through the ceiling, having a negative business impact, much like Bang and Olufsen had experienced when it was all about design. They had

132 CONSENSUS THROUGH RECONCILIATION

discovered the market for the high-end products was small because many people did not feel they needed many of the features provided, and they were unable or unwilling to pay for them.

Mr. Mantovani started the discussion by flatly stating that design people must be allowed to produce the best. Daniels felt like reminding him that a lot more Fords were sold than Ferraris but thought better of it. He really needed the cooperation of each of the members to sell their strategies to the employees in the countries they operate in. Besides, the organization recognized the value placed on the best possible designs in their Italian operation and had been careful to do design work there only when the product competed on design quality rather than price.

But this issue had become a critical one as Qwenchy decentralized its R&D activities, creating units around the world. This had led to global teams, consisting of specialists from different countries working on product development and enhancements. Daniels remembered that the "global relay team" approach had become very popular; it was, after all, a very compelling strategy on paper. But much like a relay team at a track meet, much of the success was determined by the passing of the baton. And when one shift passed their work onto the next team, there were numerous issues: language, technical approach and, of course, cultural differences. If one of the design teams was measured by their local manager on product cost leadership, another on product appearance and yet another on technical excellence, there would certainly be different priorities when designs were being created. These teams required competent leadership in order to ensure that the product did not end up being an amalgamation of inconsistent parts (the horse designed by a committee that looked like a merger between a horse, a camel and several extinct species).

Another challenge arose when performance of the team was evaluated and rewarded. Would it be assumed that overall performance would be measured and that all team members would

CONSENSUS THROUGH RECONCILIATION 133

receive the same performance rating on that basis? Or would management attempt to measure differences in individual contributions? And would rewards be distributed on an egalitarian basis or based on relative individual contributions? Certainly cultural differences would predispose members to expect different strategies. They could, of course, lock the members in a room with the award pool in the middle of the room and let them settle it. But could people with different cultural orientations ever come to consensus that all would accept?

The group moved on to the final issue. The majority of employees in many countries were operating and administrative support people, generally paid an hourly wage, with little or no variable compensation. Although there were some output-based incentives in place for production personnel in some locations, there were no "shared destiny" variable pay plans for them. In order to encourage employees to offer suggestions for improving productivity and quality and to work cooperatively, Daniels really believed in having a profit-sharing or performance-sharing plan. Such a plan would give people a reward for achieving the group/unit and organizational goals and would encourage them to contribute to the effectiveness of their fellow workers.

Lincoln Electric had used gain-sharing and individual incentives successfully for decades and had transported their plans to operations outside the U.S. However, in some cultures, the results focus caused the plans to meet resistance. Rather than attempt to modify their rewards strategy, the company withdrew from the locations where the plans were not accepted. Daniels had been impressed with their adherence to their management principles but wondered whether there was not some way to customize strategies in a way that still conformed to the organization's principles.

The group readily agreed that appropriate strategies for support people differed dramatically across locations and that the local management should be given the freedom to customize strategies

134   CONSENSUS THROUGH RECONCILIATION

to fit local realities and customs. Because it would be very unusual to transfer support people across locations and since there was little communication between them across locations, everyone seemed to buy in to the local approach.

As an overall strategy globally, the consultant had suggested to Daniels that the company could adopt profit-/performance-sharing plans that determined award pools based on organization/unit performance but that the approach used to allocate awards could be customized so there was a fit to local culture. The consultant had suggested a list of alternative allocation methods and encouraged Daniels to see whether different approaches could not accomplish the culture fit objective. The alternative distribution methods were evaluated to see where each would best fit. (See Figure 14.3.)

Daniels had expected the task force members from collectivist cultures to select the "equal dollars" or "equal percentage of pay" alternatives, those from individualistic cultures to opt for the "based on individual performance" alternative and those from high-power distance cultures to select the "varied based on organizational level" option. After a lengthy discussion, it turned out that people's opinions were much more nuanced. One of Daniel's staff members had told him that recent research studies had suggested that the differences between national cultures was more moderate than had been generally thought when it came to issues like paying for performance.[2] The consensus was that the award pools should be

> • Equal percentage of current base pay
> • Equal percentage of range midpoint
> • Equal percentage up to maximum
> • Varied based on organizational level
> • Equal dollars to each individual
> • Equal dollars per hour worked
> • Based on individual performance

Figure 14.3 Alternative Distribution Methods from Award Funds

CONSENSUS THROUGH RECONCILIATION 135

distributed in a more egalitarian manner for support personnel and that performance should be at least one of the allocation factors for management and professional personnel.

At the end of the discussion, Mr. Khasmi and Mr. Klaus, who had been conferring with each other, suggested that each local manager be given permission to allocate the award funds as they saw fit, after submitting their approach to corporate HR accompanied by a rationale for their decision. This seemed to please everyone, and Daniels could go back to headquarters and say that everyone was in agreement on the "significant" provisions. Daniels wished to get the approval of the CFO as a matter of good form. He figured the only issue for the CFO would be how much was being spent in each operation, with less concern about how. Better to tell part of the truth than to start a fight.

When Daniels got back from the task force meeting, he found the reception at headquarters a bit chilly. "So you pretty much turned the GMs loose to do what they think is right, rather than what is consistent with corporate culture?" asked Thirst, the CEO.

Daniels was concerned about this reaction because his own performance appraisal was due shortly (they evaluated each other). "We felt that the guiding principles that were critical could still be adhered to, while the local management customized the administration of the programs so they were viewed as fair and acceptable by their employees," responded Daniels. "Their perceptions about appropriateness will in the end determine whether the programs have the desired motivational impact."

Apparently, Thirst had recently found that local practices had drifted from what had been mutually agreed to in many locations, and this had put him on edge. Daniels realized that if Thirst felt it necessary to have a show of power and to rein GMs back in, the approach the task force had agreed to may seem to be a step backward. But he took a deep breath and made his pitch. "We can define the guiding principles that must be adhered to and do so in a way that makes it clear they are not negotiable. But allowing a GM to allocate award funds in a manner that is compatible with local culture and that respects local laws and taxation rules will enable them to get the best result out of the expenditure. After all, the local unit earned the funds based on measures established by corporate, so it is not ceding authority to challenge them to distribute the funds in the optimal manner."

"Perhaps," Thirst responded, "but help me communicate this in a manner that doesn't suggest we are turning the institution over to the inmates." Daniels thought that perhaps other wording might be used to describe the process of increasing GM autonomy over incentive award allocations.

Notes

1. Robert J. Greene, *Rewarding Performance: Guiding Principles; Custom Strategies,* Routledge, 2010.
2. B. Gerhart, "Compensation and National Culture," in *Global Compensation,* Routledge, 2008.

15
SUSTAINING THE EFFECTIVENESS OF THE CULTURE

Daniels wanted to do an assessment of Qwenchy's culture, now that the organization had matured and had "gone global." When they had done their original assessment using the THT Consulting cultural model early in the company's life, the executive team all agreed they wanted to keep their culture appropriate for the context they operated within and effective in achieving their goals. Daniels wanted to do two things: first, have a management symposium on culture and, second, reconvene the global task force that he had been using to globalize HR programs in order to gain their perspectives.

The management symposium was held a week later, after receiving the support of Thirst. Daniels started by relating the experience he had with doing a cultural assessment when he had been with the consulting firm.

> I worked with a utility that had been a regulated monopoly for fifty years. Their focus was on making budget and seemed relatively indifferent to customer satisfaction, since customers have no viable alternative. An automaker in a very competitive industry, with three times the capacity that demand would dictate, would almost certainly have a different attitude about the importance of customer satisfaction.

138 THE EFFECTIVENESS OF THE CULTURE

Where an organization is on this aspect of its culture may fit the realities of the past (monopolistic power), but current events (deregulation) may well alter the "should be" answer on this dimension from a singular focus on making the numbers to one of considering the customer. The utility, after discovering the need to reshape its culture, began to do so, and it evaluated its human resource management strategies in light of the cultural assessment. It found that it needed to begin hiring different types of people, to train them differently, to measure their performance using different factors and to reward them for doing different things. It also realized there was a need to take into account the cultural orientation of applicants.

Daniels believed Qwenchy should start its evaluation of its culture by identifying the significant gaps between what the culture is and what it should be. Once the gaps are identified, the impact of closing them (or consequences of not doing so) should be evaluated and then compared to the resources required to accomplish this transition. This would provide an agenda for focusing efforts on reshaping those aspects of the culture that needed to be changed.

Daniels provided the management team with an example: An assessment of the utility he had just described had identified the following gaps:

1. Performance must be defined as satisfying the customer while making the numbers.
2. The performance of the overall organization must be considered by managers when making decisions rather than only considering how their unit will be impacted.
3. Managers must balance risk with costs when making decisions.
4. Employees must be viewed as assets to invest in rather than as a line item in the budget.

THE EFFECTIVENESS OF THE CULTURE 139

5. Pay levels and pay actions must be earned through performance rather than being an entitlement that is based on time spent on the job.

The findings from the analysis at the utility had uncovered a number of undesirable realities. Departmental fiefdoms existed, causing managers to make their goals no matter what impact it had on other departments or the overall organization. Managers were indifferent to the costs of holding large inventories because they had been trained to avoid stock outs or other "failures." Investment in training was insufficient because the costs of training went against each unit's budget, and no credit was given for developing people, particularly for progression to greater responsibilities. Finally, pay adjustments equal to cost-of-living increases or increases in average wage levels (whichever was greater) were viewed as an entitlement and were given to everyone in the form of general increases and time-based step increases. When the results had been absorbed, employee and manager focus groups worked to develop recommendations for changing human resource management systems in a way that would facilitate reshaping the culture. These included: (1) changing performance criteria to include satisfying customers and positively impacting the effectiveness of other employees and other units, (2) directing and funding training out of a corporate function and budget account, (3) hiring people experienced in satisfying customers, (4) teaching employees about the economics of the business and how they impacted results and (5) modifying the base pay system to reward merit rather than just length of service.

Daniels knew the results of cultural assessments would be unique to each specific organizational culture. An assessment of another regulated utility might produce an entirely different definition of culture and/or different prescriptions. The example has been provided to illustrate the process but does not suggest that an assessment of Qwenchy's culture would produce similar results.

140 THE EFFECTIVENESS OF THE CULTURE

Daniels conveyed what he had learned by working with the global team: When an organization operates internationally, it becomes more difficult to fashion a culture that is appropriate globally. For example, if a U.S.-based organization believes unions are undesirable and expends considerable energy avoiding them, it may encounter great resistance and even legal obstacles in Germany and other countries where unions are mandated. And the governance structure in some countries consist of two-tier boards and codetermination (between management and employees). An organization that emphasizes individual incentives may find that aspect of its culture to present problems in societies that are collectivist in their orientation and in countries where governance takes a different form.

The fundamental question is whether the transnational should modify its organizational culture to align with the local societal culture, or should it maintain a globally consistent culture? As Trompenaars has suggested in *Managing People Across Cultures*,[1] there are great variations among individuals within societal cultures. So how does the organization with an individualistic culture hire Japanese nationals who are less collectivist than the norm in the operation in Japan and retain its individualistic point of view? This decision will have a profound influence on how the organization reconciles the global–local dilemma relative to defining, measuring and rewarding performance. So Qwenchy faces the same type of decision when contemplating the type of culture it wishes to have in the future and how that culture can be reconciled with the culture of the organization you are considering as a partner. The need to reconcile the cultures will vary, depending on whether you choose to make the arrangement an acquisition, a merger or an alliance. The choices are (1) impose the culture you have or want, (2) move toward the culture of the partner or (3) select the best features of both cultures and create a third culture that incorporates the best features of the two existing cultures.

THE EFFECTIVENESS OF THE CULTURE 141

Daniels suggested they move cautiously toward locking in a corporate-wide culture that might not work as well in other countries as it would in the U.S. "We learned a lot of lessons about assuming that what works here will work there when we attempted to launch the common performance and rewards management strategy. And when we considered modifying how we managed and rewarded performance to reflect differences in the types of employees, we relearned those lessons." Several of the executives at headquarters had resisted Daniel's message, since they believed that every organization should have a single culture. Daniels agreed with them that the overarching values and beliefs could be universal but felt that how they were implemented in the way people were managed across the globe might need to be customized. Lacking a consensus, he requested support for a review of the culture by a cross-national team, much as he had done with the performance and rewards management strategy and methodology. He was given the go-ahead with that initiative, although he also had marching orders to ensure that the HR strategy and programs promoted the changes in the culture that the assessment had suggested. That he supported wholeheartedly.

Reactions of the Team

Daniels began the first meeting with a dinner at which everyone was encouraged to reacquaint themselves with one another and to give the group a report on what had transpired in their countries since the last time the group had met. He felt that their work would help clarify the direction the organization would move in relative to refining its culture.

"Perhaps we could start by discussing your assessments of our current culture and your ideas about what should change," Daniels suggested. "Then we could compare your views about how the culture could be reshaped to be a better fit to your context. Management had been shocked that this team had as much difficulty as it did with a common performance and rewards management

142 THE EFFECTIVENESS OF THE CULTURE

system. But they feel that the culture of the organization would be less impacted by national cultures, so I think they expect this group to concur with the idea of a new common culture."

"But the reactions to a single system for defining and rewarding performance were a reflection of our cultural orientations, so why would management expect the response to be more positive to a homogenized organizational culture?" asked Mr. Khasmi. "Do they think the UAE operation has been thrown into a blender along with the other local cultures, resulting in a homogeneous milkshake that is less complex to deal with?"

Mr. Yakomoto added his thoughts about the issue. "We were trying very hard to be cooperative before and minimized the difficulties posed by common systems, but still we were unable to believe that the system you had proposed could be implemented without great problems surfacing. "

Daniels had promised himself that he would not overreact when the group acted like a herd of cats that had overdosed on an energy drink, and he gathered his thoughts before responding:

> I believe that the experience we had with posing a common system has made us more aware of the strength of local cultures. I also think we have recognized that open dialogue among people who are not like-minded can result in a much better solution. Someone once said that no progress can be made by a group of like-minded "reasonable" people, and I have come to realize that that is likely to be true. After all, we have made substantial changes to our marketing philosophy and strategy, and we believe our responsiveness to local consumer preferences has made a major contribution to the success we have had recently in some of your markets. Please don't think the executive team is made up of Americans who believe everyone should do it the American way. They want to be successful and are not wedded to a homogeneous approach to managing. But unless we want to be a

THE EFFECTIVENESS OF THE CULTURE 143

loose collection of national entities, we must at least have common overarching beliefs and values to guide our efforts.

Mr. Klaus supported Daniels in this matter:

I know you think we Germans want everything to be structured and predictable, but we are not so foolish as to think that people of very different cultural orientations will accept the idea that we should share a common culture, whatever that means. Let us agree on what we define as an organizational culture. I suggest the definition that Edgar Schein proposed is very wise. How we deal with problems of external adaptation and internal integration will determine whether or not our culture is appropriate. Each of our organizations must deal with the challenges posed by the environments we operate within, and those environments have significant differences. If we adopt a value organization-wide that makes us more responsive to our customers, we can all relate to that, although the differences in our customer bases will often result in different strategies. But the value is still shared organization-wide. We seem to be more concerned here about integration among ourselves, but that is more about the differences in the way we serve customers rather than about the overarching value we share. So maybe the organizational culture can be much more consistent than the manner in which we use the internal management system.

Daniels asked group members to take a turn to express their views on the type of culture(s) that would fit Qwenchy overall and in their locales. Mr. Yakamoto began:

I know you all think we in Japan do everything collectively, and to some extent that is our orientation. But we are very focused on our customers and in fact believe in a "demand

144 THE EFFECTIVENESS OF THE CULTURE

pull" approach rather than pushing products we wish to sell. So the value that prescribes a customer focus would be very desirable, since we are already well down that path. I worry more about the approach to defining and measuring performance that Qwenchy has used in the past. Everything defined and measured at the individual level, assuming that if every person performs well, the organization will also do well. But that is the "push" mentality. We in Japan define what is required at the organizational level and then let that determine what we expect from units and individuals, which is the "demand pull" approach. If work groups choose to carry people who are currently not contributing adequately, we are less inclined to step in to punish those nonperformers. We, of course, want to help them improve, and if they continue to fail to meet expectations, other steps may be necessary. The cultural assessment showed an agreement among the U.S. respondents on a move to making a portion of all rewards contingent on group/organization performance and that is encouraging, but what did our group believe?

Mr. Chan then spoke for China. "Our employees are not convinced that they are in control of outcomes in many situations and that it is wrong to reward people solely on the basis of results."

Mr. Khasmi added, "I don't want to speak out of turn, but I support that point and think the idea that everyone is rewarded only when performance is good is wrongheaded." Mr. Chan nodded, and Ms. Gupta supported them by pointing out that the environment in developing countries is much more turbulent and uncertain and that organizations are much more impacted by uncontrollable external factors than in places like the U.S. The can-do attitude prevalent in the U.S. was obviously not supported in some of their foreign operations, and Daniels felt it would be important to be sure that pay for performance was accepted as a common value. He realized,

THE EFFECTIVENESS OF THE CULTURE   145

however, that performance was being defined somewhat differently across their global operations and that those variations had been more or less sanctioned by corporate.

"I also believe that the responses to the question about what constitutes sound management make it clear this was a U.S. sample rather than a Japanese one," Mr. Yakamoto added. "Although we have always believed leadership is important, we believe managers are responsible for the success of their subordinates and that they have a responsibility for their success. Mr. Klaus and I disagree on that point, I know, since we had a discussion about it recently. I do not believe the German approach is wrong, but we in Japan have a different view about hierarchy and what determines the position in that hierarchy an individual is placed in."

Ms. Gupta added support for Yakamoto's point:

> There has been a lot written about the "Indian way" lately, much of it based on substantive research.[2] The actions of our leaders in the corporate arena demonstrates a strong concern for the impact of organizations on society and on the development of India and its people. Much of this is driven by Hindi principles that motivate leaders to include contribution to society in their objectives. And we believe in a holistic engagement by our employees, in order to sustain morale and build a productive culture. We understand that Qwenchy must serve its shareholders, but we do not rank shareholder interests as highly as the executives at the corporate office. We view our people as assets to be developed, not costs to be reduced, and it is not weakness that causes us to shy away from using staff reductions as the first reaction to declining revenues. A recent study found that Indian firms invested more in training new hires than most Western firms do, so it is not difficult to understand why we are reluctant to divest assets we have invested so heavily in. We use the

146   THE EFFECTIVENESS OF THE CULTURE

Hindi *jugaad*, which is finding a way around obstacles, which are frequent in our turbulent environment. What all of this means is that we believe continuous organizational learning is a requirement for survival and that it takes everyone to succeed, both in the short term and in the long term.

Mr. Mantovani started by saying that the representative of the most emotional culture had shown great restraint and had waited until all others had spoken:

Of course, that gave me a political advantage, knowing where everyone else stood. One cannot succeed in Italy without political acumen. Much of what has been said has led me to believe that, if we define corporate culture as a set of beliefs, values and principles, we can operate with a common culture. But when it comes to operating in a manner consistent with the culture, we must recognize that the diversity in local contexts requires that our guiding mantra should be "think globally and locally; act appropriately." Only a fool would believe that that will result in all of us doing things in the same way.

"Well," thought Daniels, "only a fool would believe that this was going to be easy." But he realized that they were dealing with issues at the very heart of how the organization's philosophy should be reshaped in order to ensure that the culture was a good fit for the organization and that it did not result in suboptimal performance in local operations due to conflicts with local culture.

What Daniels had come to accept was that his earlier attempt to quickly achieve a consensus on homogenizing the process of defining, measuring and rewarding performance was a mistake. As long as Qwenchy met its objectives in a manner that was consistent with its values and beliefs, as well as being legal, how each of its global

THE EFFECTIVENESS OF THE CULTURE   147

operations measured individual contributions was really not something that needed to be controlled at headquarters. He remembered the sensitivity of Mr. Khasmi about using the term "performance appraisal," which for him smacked of evaluating the worth of individuals. It also suggested the evaluator was capable of judging the person being evaluated. The emotion elicited by the word "appraisal" rendered him incapable of viewing the process as valid. However, when the phrase "contribution review" was substituted, he was able to accept that the organization should tie rewards at least partially to what one had contributed and that paying for performance was a sound principle. Although Daniels could not accept that such wordplay would make that much of a difference to some, it apparently did, so why negatively impact performance by "standing on a principle" (which, of course, was one he could accept given his own cultural orientation)?

What this had taught Daniels was that the Trompenaars three R's were important:

- *Recognize* cultural differences when they exist.
- *Respect* the beliefs and values of those who differ in their cultural orientation.
- *Reconcile* the issues that the differences cause by cultural contrasts.

Daniels felt he had learned one of the competencies of a global executive: to treat others as they would like to be treated rather than how he would like to be treated. He smiled when he pledged to himself that he would think globally *and* locally and act appropriately.

Notes

1. Fons Trompenaars and Charles Hampden-Turner, *Managing People Across Cultures*, Capstone, 2004.
2. P. Cappelli, H. Singh, J. Singh, and M. Useem, *The India Way*, Harvard Business Press, 2010

EPILOGUE

The characters used in the case were developed to illustrate different cultural orientations across countries and societies. They are not meant to be stereotypes. Based on research, the authors know that there is as much variation in cultural orientation across individuals within a culture or country as there is across cultures and countries. Yet the differences in perspectives portrayed in the book are very realistic based on actual experiences of the authors and the extensive research conducted by THT Consulting.

There is no consensus on whether globalization will cause cultures to blend, making them more alike, or whether people will hold on to the cultural orientation that resulted from how they were socialized. In some countries, immigration has resulted in ethnically consistent subpopulations, while in others there has been more adaptation by those arriving in the culture of their new home country. The U.S. has been used as an example of the so-called melting pot, but two hundred years after its founding, one can still find ethnic enclaves that resemble the country of origin rather than the country of residence.

How organizations define, measure and reward performance is one of the critical workforce management strategy decisions. Although the organization may prefer one strategy for all employees, cultural diversity in the workforce may result in differing levels of acceptance by employees. Global organizations can operate in the same way under the same rules for everyone, everywhere. Or

150   EPILOGUE

they can adapt to fit local cultures without being concerned about global consistency. A third way is to reconcile the dilemmas posed by cultural differences by using strategies that are both global and local. How this can be done has been the topic of this book.

The behavioral theories that have withstood research scrutiny in the so-called Western World (e.g., expectancy, equity and reinforcement theories) suggest that a tight linkage between employee competence, performance and rewards should produce positive motivation. But perhaps it is difficult to make pay for performance work well in some countries/cultures because these theories do not apply everywhere. Most of the research supporting these theories has been conducted on Western/Northern employees in Western/Northern organizations by Western/Northern researchers. One could therefore ask the question, "Will the findings hold up in other parts of the world?"

The impact of national/ethnic/societal cultures on the performance of an organization and the effectiveness of its workforce can be significant. It is important to identify differences among contrasting cultures so that organizations can anticipate the impact of these differences and search for ways to reconcile the resulting conflicts. This can be done by defining opposites, recognizing the values associated with each and determining how the differences can be reconciled. But thought processes suitable for dealing with paradox must then be utilized: For example, "How can we ensure recognition of the group's performance through identifying individual contributions? And then, how can we recognize individual contributions through the group and the group's performance?" This type of circular logic is an anathema to some cultures—but it can be used to ensure that basic assumptions of one culture (e.g., the Anglo Saxon viewpoint) are not accepted without considering the assumptions prevailing in other cultures.

If a workforce is expected to be motivated to do what the organization needs, employees must believe that performance and rewards

EPILOGUE 151

are managed appropriately, competitively and equitably. It has become apparent to many organizations that one model for defining, measuring and rewarding performance may be a poor fit for the new environmental realities. And given the complexity of many organizations, it may be inadvisable to define, measure and reward performance in the same manner for all types of their employees.[1] Coauthor Greene posits that there are common principles that, if adhered to, can guide the development of effective performance and rewards management strategies and programs. But coauthor Trompenaars concludes from his extensive cross-cultural research that people vary in their personal needs, values and priorities, necessitating openness to customizing strategies to fit local cultures. Additionally, different types of work require different types of contributions to organizational effectiveness. The attempt to develop a single strategy and/or program for a very diverse workforce in the pursuit of consistency and simplicity has failed in many organizations.

Einstein sagely observed that "the solution to problems should be as simple as possible . . . but no simpler." Oliver Wendell Holmes said, "I would give nothing for simplicity this side of complexity but would give everything for simplicity the other side of complexity."

The tension between common guiding principles and custom strategies is always present. A single performance and rewards management strategy can produce global consistency, and one strategy may be simpler to administer than multiple strategies. But if different categories of employee should have their performance and rewards managed differently, due to differences in the type of work they do and the contributions they make, then customized strategies that ensure a "best fit" to each local context should be considered. And if employees vary in their cultural makeup, it may not be advisable to attempt to mandate a single approach for all employees in all locations.

A potential disadvantage is associated with having different human resource strategies for different employee groups. This approach can create perceptions that someone else is getting a better deal or, even worse, that some employees are being discriminated against. The laws and regulations in many countries mandate that different treatments of different types of employees be justified as a business necessity. An even more critical, concern should be the potential loss of critical skills or reduced productivity, due to employee dissatisfaction caused by inappropriate strategies. The challenges associated with localized strategies must be recognized and compared to the potential advantages. The one-vs.-many-strategies balancing act is a difficult one. Trompenaars refers to the balancing process as reconciling dilemmas.

The performance and rewards management strategies that have been the most widely used by developed Western countries are being questioned, even within the West. This is in part due to changes in the employment arrangement. Historically, the assumption was that employees would spend most or all of their careers in one organization. Today's reality is that strategies should recognize the increased mobility of people across organizations, and separation can be initiated by either party. Strategies for managing performance and rewards have been impacted by this change in employer–employee expectations. New strategies are needed to better fit mobile and diverse workforces. Yet many organizations persist in attempting to make one performance management model and one rewards strategy fit the entire workforce.

Clearly the perception that strategies do not fit current realities has been fueled by the realization that the environment looks very different today than it did one or two decades ago, while performance and rewards strategies have not changed much. But change in the environment does not automatically render strategies ineffective. For this reason, strategists must not assume that environmental changes mandate strategy changes. On the other hand, scanning the environment continuously is necessary due to its dynamic nature, and when strategy shifts are mandated, they certainly should be made. This is even more critical as workforces become increasingly diverse.

Performance and rewards management are inextricably woven together. The yin-yang symbol in Figure E.1 illustrates the relationship between performance and rewards management. The two are facets of a whole, which is the process of defining, measuring and rewarding performance in a manner that will contribute to workforce effectiveness. The two must be in harmony and are indispensable to each other. When aligned, they produce a synergistic effect. Alter one, and the other is affected. Treating performance management and rewards management as separate activities can result in a lack of integration.

Figure E.1 The Yin-Yang of Performance and Rewards Management

154 EPILOGUE

Formulating guiding principles and developing specific strategies should both be done in an informed manner—informed both by theory and by evidence based on research and on experience. The research in the field of organizational behavior provides useful theory that points decision makers to principles that can be used to develop strategies. The management literature provides evidence as to what makes strategies and programs work or not work, as well as identifying the contextual factors that seem to impact their effectiveness. The cultural anthropology literature provides considerable insight into the impact of culture on the effectiveness and appropriateness of alternative strategies. All of this evidence should be applied when deciding how to define, measure and reward performance in a specific situation. Human resource practitioners and line managers all too often make decisions that are based on faulty or outdated assumptions.

The story told in this book has illustrated the issues that will arise when people with differing cultural orientations attempt to agree on how people should be managed. Common strategies, programs and processes for rewarding performance may be effective across cultures if consensus can be achieved and if those affected by them view them as equitable, competitive and appropriate. Each organization must decide how to achieve that acceptance.

Note

1. Robert J. Greene, *Rewarding Performance: Guiding Principles: Custom Strategies,* Routledge, 2010.

INDEX

Italic indicates a table or figure on the corresponding page.

abstract ideas, focus 42
accountability, expectation 95
accounting cycle, time frames 125
achievement: ascription, reconciliation 104; development, usage 99–100; orientation, religion (correlation) 100; reconciliation, ascription perspectives (usage) 99
achieving society 100
affective cultures: emotions, availability/expression 76–7; reward systems, focus 77
affective perspectives, usage 73
AMD: codevelopment 111–12; co-opetition spirit 69–70
American dream, representation 52
Americans, Lewin perspective 82
Applied Materials, codevelopment programs (usage) 111–12
appraisal: concrete facts, usage 36; criteria 34; criteria, evaluation 36; fair company norms, basis 36; focus 36; principles *see* staff; process, guidelines 35; ratings 76–7; systems, attention 67
ascription: achievement, reconciliation 104; orientation 99; perspectives, usage 99
authority: deference, orientation 117; impact 119
award funds: allocation 135; distribution methods (alternatives) *134*

balanced scorecard: concept 95; dangers/benefits, examples *115*; example *94*; linear restrictions, overcoming 113–14
Bang & Olufsen: design, impact 131–2; market challenges 112–13
bankruptcy 4
base pay system, modification 139
"beating around the bush" 92
behavioral theories 150

156 INDEX

being, doing (contrast) *101*
being-oriented cultures 100
best fit, ensuring 151–2
best practices, learning *51*
brainstorming 33–4
Brink, Nina 68
bureaucracy: disappearance 10; impact 6
bureaucratic cultures, impact 119
business: controlled/expressive orientation, differences (implication) 75; control perspectives, implications 108–11; deal, neutral objective aspects (addressing) 92; economics, employees (teaching) 139; partner/strangers, understanding (strategies) 91–6; relationships 81

candidate personalities, assessment tools (THT Consulting) 22–3
centralization, low degree 4
change, effecting 12, *14*
circling round *92*
client satisfaction, improvement 70
coaching 3
Coca-Cola, American dream representation 52
codevelopment programs, usage 111–12
cohesion, source *13*
collective goals, agreement (pressure) 62
Collective Labour Agreement, Phillips breakage 67

collectivist orientation 59
collectivist perspectives, findings 61–2
collectivist perspectives, individualistic perspectives: contrast 59–64; reconciliation 57
comments, impact 85–7
communication, richness/baggage 91–2
company, global strategy adoption 49
competition, confrontation 32
concentric circles 87–8
concrete facts, usage 36
conflict: escalation 86; signals 109
consensus: absence 141; achievement, reconciliation (usage) 127; modification 62
consistency: flexibility, contrast *43*; organizational focus 123
consistency-focused disapproval 44
control: impact, example 114–15; locus, measurement scale 106–8; perspectives, implications 108–11; principle *13*
controlled, expressive (contrast) *74*
controlled orientation, expressive orientation (contrast) 75
controlled points of view, expressed points of view (reconciliation) 78–80
control orientation 74; culture differences, assessment process 106–8
control-oriented cultures 75
cooperation, competition 67–72
co-opetition 67–72; spirit 69–70

INDEX

corporate culture: examples 2–3; international variation *see* preferred corporate cultures
cost-of-living increases 139
creative people, characteristics *23*
cross-cultural research, impact 151
cross-integration 112
cultural anthropology literature, insight 154
cultural assessments, results 139–40
cultural commonality, acceptance 143
cultural differences: assessment process 106–8; impact 30
cultural diversity, impact 32
cultural orientation: acceptance; assessment 46
cultures: control-oriented cultures 75; creation *see* desired culture; decision making 63–4; defining/ placement 21; effectiveness, sustaining 137; Eiffel Tower Culture 5–11; emotional expression, assessment 73–5; expression-oriented cultures 75; Family Culture 3–4; globalized context 29; Guided Missile Culture 4–5; ignoring 48; impact, insight 154; Incubator Culture 4; local cultures 142–3; management symposium, holding 137–8; organizational cultures *3, 10*; orientation, difference 59–60; partner/ strangers, understanding

(strategies) 91–6; pattern 2; power/persistence 1; status orientation, measurement process 100–4; strategies, effectiveness/ineffectiveness 128; universalistic perspectives, particularistic perspectives (contrast) 41–52
cultures, differences 74; patterns 11–18; testing process 88–90
current ratings, past ratings (impact) 122
customer satisfaction 138; tracking 131

decentralized control, impact 5
decision, implementation (disparity) 63
decision making: basis 122; duration 62; *see also* cultures
demand pull approach 144
Deming, W. Edwards 16, 95
departmental fiefdoms, impact 139
deregulation 138
design people, freedom 132
desired culture, creation 19
destiny, control (belief) 108
differences: patterns 11–18; reconciliation 48
diffuse cultures: reconciliation, integrated scorecard (usage) 96–7; report writing 93
diffuse orientation 85; G-type 83; losing face 81; specific orientation, difference (recognition) 86–7

diffuse-oriented cultures, specific/diffuse orientations (differences) 87

diffuse-oriented person, answers 92

diffuse perspectives, specific perspectives (reconciliation) 81

dilemmas (reconciliation), individual propensity (determination) 27

Dilemma Theory 25–6

disapproval: consistency-focused disapproval 44; flexibility-focused disapproval 44–6

discrimination, claim 95

dissenters, voting down (unacceptability) 62

doing approach 100

doing, being (contrast) *101*

dress code, orientation differences 85

duty, concept (importance) 6

economic development, usage 99–100

egalitarian perspectives, hierarchical perspectives (reconciliation) 117

egalitarian structure, authority (impact) 119

Eiffel Tower Culture 5–11; cultural vices 10; Incubator Culture, relationship 9; persistence 10; positive aspects, adoption 19; quadrant support 16; relationship 7

Eiffel Tower organization, usage 16

Einstein, Albert 151

email, example *33*

emerging organizations, growth 21

emotional culture 146

emotional expression: assessment 73–5; findings 74

emotions: availability/expression 76–7; showing 74

employees: asset perspective 138; confrontation, Japanese avoidance 95; goals establishment 118; longevity, higher pay 103–4; operating/administrative positions 133; pay rate/ranges 103; performance, appraisal 102, 122; performance, motivation 110; reward methods 17; teaching 139

entrepreneurship 34

environment: organizational operation 111; response, focus 109

equal dollars alternatives, selection 134

equality-hierarchical axis: contrasts *12*; human resources, role 12

Equality-Hierarchical axis, contrasts 11

equal percentage of pay alternatives, selection 134

ethnic cultures, impact 150

Europe, control orientation 74

excellence, definition *13*

executives, long-term incentives 128–9

expatriates: assignments, extension 129–30; rewards packages, resentment 130; usage 30, 130

INDEX

expressed points of view, controlled points of view (reconciliation) 78–80

expression-oriented cultures 75

expressive, controlled (contrast) *74*

expressive cultures, reward systems (focus) 77

expressive orientation, controlled orientation (contrast) 75

external adaptation, problem 1

external control: internal control, contrast *107*; orientation 105, 106, 110; sense 108–9

external controlled orientation, internal controlled orientation (differences) 106

external customers: focus, dilemma 111–12; internal processes, contrast 112–16

external factors, control (absence) 144–5

externally controlled perspectives, internally controlled perspectives (reconciliation) 105

fair company norms, basis 36

Family Culture 3–4; impact 8–9; shortcomings 19; usage, example 14–15

Feeling: preference, test 24; thinking, contrast *24, 25*

feelings, openness 73–5

financial crisis (2007-2012), reasons 68

Five Dragons, success 61

flexibility, consistency (contrast) *43*

flexibility-focused disapproval 44–6

Florida, Richard 17

forced choice question 24

Ford, Henry 6

Fordism, reality 7–8

formalization: high degree 6; low degree 4

function-specific behavior 36, 79

future orientation 121–2

gain-sharing incentives, usage 133

global corporation, cultures (ignoring) 48

globalization, process 46

global-local dilemma 140

global-local tension/reconciliation *50*

global organization *128*; operation 149–50

global relay team approach 132

global strategy, adoption 49

goals 34; agreement, pressure *see* collective goals; establishment, employee role 118; setting 12, *14*

Godfather, The 76

good fit determinations 22

group-oriented cultures, decision making 62

groups: attention 71; behaviors, examination 70; incentives 126; orientation, individual orientation (contrast) *63*; preferences 45

G-type circles 88

Guided Missile Culture 4–5; appropriateness 15; benefits 19; group, impact 8

guiding principles, importance 135
guiding star *13*

Hampden-Turner, Charles 25
harmony, seeking 109
Hawthorne Experiments 6–8
Heineken, managerial training 51–2
hierarchical perspectives,
    egalitarian perspectives
    (reconciliation) 117
hierarchy, perspective 145
high-context perspectives,
    low-context perspectives
    (reconciliation) 91
high-context, report writing 93
high-potential people, neglect
    (perceptions) 94
Hindi principles 145–6
Holmes, Oliver Wendell 151
Hong Kong, success 61
human resources (HR): case
    study 31–3; initiatives 127;
    interventions, quadrants *14*;
    letter, example 33–5;
    principles *13*; role 12; strategies,
    differences (disadvantages) 152;
    tools, effectiveness (factors)
    17–18
human resources management
    (HRM) 6; systems, change 139;
    values/beliefs 9
humor, impact 75–8

I (uppercase spelling) 64
IAP *see* InterCultural Leadership
    Assessment Profiling

ideas, generation 15
improvement, organizational
    focus 123
incentives: differences 21; gain-
    sharing incentives, usage
    133; group incentives 126;
    individual incentives, usage 133;
    organization-wide incentives
    126; output-based incentives
    133; plans, operation 110–11
Incubator Culture 4
India, emotions (showing) 74
Indian way, perspective 145–6
individual freedom, opting
    (percentage) *60*
individual incentives:
    organizational emphasis 140;
    plans, impact 65–6; usage 133
individualistic cultures, I
    (uppercase spelling) 64
individualistic orientation 59
individualistic perspectives,
    collectivist perspectives: contrast
    59–64; reconciliation 57
individualistic perspectives,
    findings 61–2
individual orientation, group
    orientation (contrast) *63*
individual-oriented cultures,
    decision making 62–3
individuals: cultural orientation,
    assessment 46; function-specific
    behavior 58; opinions, respect
    62; pay-for-performance 58–9;
    position 145; results 58
inner-directed orientation 111

INDEX

inshallah (Islamic belief) 104
integrated scorecard: approach
113–14; example *94*; usage 96–7
Integrated Type Indicator (ITI)
26; questions 27
Intel: codevelopment 111–12;
co-opetition spirit 69
intercultural competence,
confirmation 46
InterCultural Leadership
Assessment Profiling (IAP)
42, 46
interculture overlap, implication 31
internal control: culture, behavioral
research 110; external control,
contrast *107*; orientation 105,
106; score 108; sense 108
internal controlled orientation,
external controlled orientation
(differences) 106
internal integration, problem 1
internally controlled perspectives,
externally controlled perspectives
(reconciliation) 105
internal management system,
usage 143–4
internal processes: external
customers, contrast 112–16;
focus, dilemma 111–12
internationalization process 68–9
international organization,
compromise 48–9
intraculture diversity, implication 31
intuition, thinking (transition
effectiveness) 22–3
irony, impact 75–8

Japan: emotions, showing
(unacceptability) 74; evasion/
noncommittal approach 95; face,
maintenance 83–4; nationals,
hiring 140; success 61
job-related results 53, 77
judging, perceiving (oscillation) 23
jugaad 146

KLM-Alitalia alliance, success 47
Knutsen, Anders 113
KSLA, Shell experiment 69–70

Latin Europe, control orientation 74
leaders: development *14*;
motivation 145–6
leadership: competence, requirement
132; functions, shift 50
"lean and mean" cost-cutting,
impact 114
Lewin, Kurt 51, 82–3; G-type
circles 88; misperceptions, sources
88; personality, concentric circles
87–8; U-type circles 87
life space, permeation 87
Likert scales 27
Lincoln Electric, gain-sharing/
individual incentives, usage 133
linear scales 26–7
local cultures: perspective 142;
strength, awareness 142–3
local management, impact 135–6
local practices, shift 135–6
locus of control, measurement
scale 106–8
logic, types 24

long-term incentives 128–9; plans, usage 126

long-term performance, cultural emphasis 126

long-term perspectives, short-term perspectives (reconciliation) 125

losing face 81, 83–4

low-context cultures, impact 92

low-context perspectives, high-context perspectives (reconciliation) 91

low context, report writing 93

Malpensa Airport, development (prepayment) 47

management: contributions 5; control 68; development programs (THT Consulting) 93; process, modification 141; quality, defining 145; style *13*; symposium, holding 137–8

managers: expectations 76; task avoidance, percentage *89*; task relationship, segregation 82, 87

Managing People Across Cultures (Trompenaars) 140

market pull: approach 112; strategies 109

markets: evolution, understanding 112–13; maturity 15

matrixed structures, usage 130

McDonald's, globalization/consistency 52

measurement time frame: dilemma, reconciliation 126; establishment 125

melting pot 149

mentoring 3

merit pay 65–6; programs, connection 124; systems, performance reward 126

Middle East, control orientation 74

misperceptions, sources 88

misunderstanding, basis 86

money, usage 12

monopolistic power 138

motivation 118, 145–6; expectation 150–1; impact 109–10

multicultural teams, impact 69

multilocal organization 48

multilocal particularistic approach 49–50

multinationalism, richness/complexity 50

multinationals, expatriates (usage) 30

national cultures: differences, testing 88–90; impact 150

National Semiconductor, co-opetition spirit 69–70

nature: mechanistic nature 108; organic view 108

nepotism 41

neutral (reconciliation), affective perspectives (usage) 73

neutral cultures, managerial expectations 76

New Economy 67–8

new science, incubation 8

obligations, focus 42–3

optimal organizational culture, determination 1

INDEX

163

organizational cultures: modification 140; relationship *3*; typologies, characteristics *10*

organizations: culture, importance 22; direction 141–2; growth 21; international operation, impact 140; international organization 48–9; learning process 16–17; management, problem solving perspective 5; multilocal organization 48; outcomes, desire 109–10; performance, managerial consideration 138; resources, provision 109; results 68; rewards, bases 54–5; service, valuation 103–4; subcultures, creation (necessity) 20; transnational organization 49–52

organization-wide incentives 126

orientation: abandonment 48; ascription orientation 99; differences (dress code) 85; diffuse orientation 85; external control orientation 105; internal control orientation 105; specific orientation 84–5

output-based incentives 133

paralysis by analysis 114

Partek, financial surplus (reservation) 93

particularistic orientation 53

particularistic perspectives: reconciliation 39; universalistic perspectives, contrast 41–6

partner/strangers, understanding (strategies) 91–6

past distortions, repetition 122

past orientation 121

past performance: consistency/ improvement, organizational focus 123

past performance, consideration 123

pay awards, performance basis *129*

pay-for-performance scheme, development (example) 68–9

pay-for-performance value, acceptance 144–5

pay levels/actions, earning 139

pay rate/ranges 103

people: diffuse orientation 85; high-potential people, neglect (perceptions) 94; hiring 139; person-oriented culture, characterization 4; salespeople, strategy (decision) 131; specific orientation 84–5

performance: basis *129*; criteria, change 139; culture, formation 99–100; defining/measurement, aggregate level 64; defining/ measurement/reward, organizational process 30–1; defining/measurement/reward, process (homogenization) 146–7; defining, past sales percentage (basis) 122; design/measurement/ reward 22; development, guidance (principles) 151; evaluation, status (impact) 102; improvement 8–9; individualistic definition/

collectivist definition, dilemma 64–5; measurement 12, *14*; measures, adjustment 130; motivation 12, *14*; organizational defining/ measurement/reward, aggregate level 66; organizational definitions 94–5; pay-for-performance 58–9; performance-sharing plans, adoption 134; ratings 103; results, rating basis 36; subjective judgments, usage 129; yin-yang *153*

performance appraisal 52–3, 76–7, 102, 147; top-down process 117–18

performance management: challenge 95; global imposition 110; model *20*; strategies 152; systems, components 118

Personal Intelligent Communicator, design 85–6

personality: concentric circles 87–8; G-type circles 88; misperceptions, sources 88; U-type circles 87–8

perspectives, reconciliation 121

Phillips: Collective Labour Agreement breakage 67; product marketing, struggle 112

Player of the Game 66

power: monopolistic power 138; orientation *13*

preferred corporate cultures, international variation 17–18

present orientation 121

privacy: danger zone 83; public, danger zone *84*

product: appearance, impact 132; designs, creation 131–2; planning, feedback 112

production personnel, output-based incentives 133

productivity, feedback 8

profiling tools (THT concerns) 23–4

profit-sharing plans: adoption 134; impact 124

promotion, procedures (links) 35

proposals, craziness (perspective) 86

Protestantism, impact 99–100

public information/privacy, danger zone *84*

push mentality 144

quality circle, examples *15, 16*

quality of life, impact *101*

questions, diffuse-oriented person answers 92

realistic job previews (RJPs), usage 22

Recognize Respect Reconcile (3Rs) 147

reconciliation, possibility 53–4

religion, achievement orientation (correlation) 100

report writing 93

representation 62–3

research and development (R&D): activities, decentralization 132;

INDEX

feedback 112; team, idea presentation 83

return-on-investment targets, organizational setting 122

Rewarding Performance: Guiding Principles; Custom Strategies 127

rewards: aggregate level, dilemma 66–7; dilemma, reconciliation 77–8; individual level, dilemma 66–7; individual orientation, group orientation (contrast) *61*; organizational basis 110–11; procedures, links 35; programs, impact 65–6; strategy, selection 119; systems, attention 67; systems, focus 77; trickle down 119

rewards management: strategy 141; yin-yang *153*

rigid hierarchy 119

Rise of the Creative Class, The (Florida) 17

risk/costs, managerial balance 138

role-orientated culture, characterization 5–11

Rotter, J.B. 106; scale, usage 107

sales, impact (understanding) 130–1

salespeople, strategy (decision) 131

sales personnel, short-term incentives 128–9

satisfaction 118

Schein, Edgar 1

scientific sleep 7

scorecard, balancing (dangers/ benefits) *115*

Sematech (cooperative institution) 69

service, valuation 103–4

Seven Cultures of Capitalism, The (Trompenaars) 84

shared destiny: mind-set, encouragement 21; variable pay plans, absence 133

shared destiny plan 66–7

shareholders, serving 145–6

Shell, KSLA experiment 69–70

short-term incentives 128–9

short-term perspectives, long-term perspectives (reconciliation) 125

short-term results, cultural emphasis 126

Singapore: emotions, showing (acceptability) 74; success 61

societal cultures, impact 150

society, individualization 69

Sony, product marketing 112

South Korea, success 61

Spain, face (maintenance) 83–4

specifically oriented cultures, specific/diffuse orientations (differences) 87

specific cultures: reconciliation, integrated scorecard (usage) 96–7; report writing 93

specific/diffuse, encounter 84

specific orientation 85; diffuse orientation, difference (recognition) 86–7

specific-oriented cultures, managerial task segregation 82

specific perspectives, diffuse perspectives (reconciliation) 81

spiritual justification, pursuit 99–100

staff: appraisal, principles 36–7; development *14*; rewarding 12, *14*

start-up organizations, growth 21

status 62–3; achievement/ economic development, usage 99–100; impact 102; orientation, measurement process 100–4; origin *101*

strangers, understanding (strategies) 91–6

strengths, playing to 108

subcultures, creation (necessity) 20

subjective judgments, usage 129

Sweden, control orientation 74

Taiwan, success 61

talent, attraction/retention/ motivation 12, *14*

task-oriented culture 4–5; employees, reward methods 17

task/result focus, support 79

Taylor, Frederick Winslow 6

Taylorism, reality 7–8

team: performance, evaluation/ reward challenge 132–3; reactions, example 141–7; scorecard 8; spirit, stimulation 69

technical excellence, impact 132

Ten Principles 36–7, 71–2; inapplicability, perception 78

Thinking: feeling, contrast *24, 25*; orientation, initiation 26; preference, test 24

THT Consulting: candidate assessment tool 22–3; cultural model usage 137; research 149; response divergence 44; WebCue tools 113–14

time frame, establishment 125

training, directing/funding 139

transnational firm, growth 68–9

transnational organization: logic, search 51; organizational culture, modification 140; reconciliation 49–52

transnational specialization 50

trend line, creation 124

understatement, impact 75–8

unions, U.S.-based organizational perspective 140

universalistic perspectives: particularistic perspectives, contrast 41–52; reconciliation 39

up-market offerings 113

utility, assessment (example) 138–9

U-type circles 87–8

values 34; organization-wide adoption 143–4

vertical hierarchies, bureaucratic cultures (impact) 119

volume manufacturing, disappearance 10

voting, occurrence (frequency) 62

wage levels, increases 139
WebCue tools 113–14
Weber, Max 6
Western countries, internal control score 108
work: doing, importance 65; feelings, open expression 73–5; repetition 94–5

workforce: cultural diversity 29, 118–19; management strategies 30; motivation, expectation 150–1
World Online 68

yin-yang: logic type 24; symbol *153*